GREAT AMERICAN

FOR
JAMES BEARD
AND JULIA CHILD,
WHO LIT THE LAMP
AND SHOWED US
THE WAY

COOKING SCHOOLS

GREAT AMERICAN COOKING SCHOOLS

American Food & California Wine
Bountiful Bread: Basics to Brioches
Christmas Feasts from History
Romantic & Classic Cakes
Cooking of the South
Dim Sum & Chinese One-Dish Meals
Fine Fresh Food—Fast
Fresh Garden Vegetables
Ice Cream & Ices
Omelettes & Soufflés
Pasta! Cooking It, Loving It
Quiche & Pâté
Soups & Salads
Successful Parties: Simple & Elegant

DIM SUM
AND
CHINESE
ONE-DISH MEALS
A CONTEMPORARY APPROACH

JEAN YUEH

ILLUSTRATED BY DONALD HENDRICKS

IRENA CHALMERS COOKBOOKS, INC. • **NEW YORK**

IRENA CHALMERS COOKBOOKS, INC.

PUBLISHER
Irena Chalmers

Sales and Marketing Director
Diane J. Kidd

Managing Editor
Jean Atcheson

Series Design
Helene Berinsky

Cover Design
Milton Glaser
Karen Skelton, *Associate Designer*

Cover Photography
Matthew Klein

Editor for this book
Anne C. Becker
Irene Rich, *Associate Editor*

Typesetting
Cosmos Press, New York

Printing
Lucas Litho, Inc., Baltimore

Editorial Offices
23 East 92nd Street
New York, NY 10028
(212) 289-3105

Sales Offices
P.O. Box 322
Brown Summit, NC 27214
(919) 656-3115

ISBN # 0-941034-05-4
© 1981 by Jean Yueh. All rights reserved.
Printed and published in the United States of America
by Irena Chalmers Cookbooks, Inc.
LIBRARY OF CONGRESS
CATALOG CARD NO.: 81-68834
   Yueh, Jean
      Dim Sum and Chinese one-dish meals.

   Greensboro, N.C.: Chalmers, Irena Cookbooks, Inc.
84 p.
8108   810722

Contents

Author's Note

The cuisine of a country is so often a reflection of that country's culture. Modern American cuisine, however—like America itself—is a blend of many cultures. This "melting pot" of the world, influenced by the foods of Europe throughout its history, has in recent years been affected by the foods of the Orient as well. And no Oriental cuisine has had greater impact on America than that of China.

Perhaps this is because Chinese culinary art, which dates back some 4,000 years, is in tune with America's present concerns about energy, nutrition and economy. And perhaps, too, it's because the traditional, and sometimes tedious, preparation of Chinese food can be simplified today with one of the marvels of Western technology—modern kitchen equipment. Cooking is a fine art that can be kept alive only if it meets the needs of changing times and lifestyles. With that in mind, I have used modern kitchen appliances where they will save time and labor—but not where they will sacrifice the authentic taste and aesthetic appearance that make classical Chinese cooking unique.

This dim sum and one-dish meal cookbook follows my philosophy of contemporary and practical approaches, using the food processor and other up-to-date appliances to create the same delectable food served in Chinese teahouses. Recipes are flexible enough for use with or without a food processor, and my instructions are easy and explicit enough for even the most inexperienced of cooks. I do not use monosodium glutamate in my recipes, for if you cook with fresh, wholesome ingredients, no artificial flavor-enhancer is necessary.

I believe that by blending the best of classical Chinese cooking with Western technology, you can achieve a fine harmony between East and West and cook better, healthier food in less time.

國以民為本．民以食為天

The nation thrives on its people.
The people thrive on food.

Introduction

Dim Sum and Chinese Teahouses

The purpose of this book is to introduce Americans to the pleasures of dim sum, a Cantonese teahouse specialty still unknown to many diners in this country. If you have never savored these delicious treats, served at Cantonese teahouses in areas with large Chinese communities, then you have missed a unique experience.

Dim sum (literally translated as "dot-the-heart") are dainty morsels stuffed with savory ingredients in a matchless variety of tastes and textures. Mostly steamed, fried or baked, they are to be consumed in a small and satisfying quantity whenever the heart and stomach most crave them. The feeling of sensuous well-being and deep satisfaction dim sum bring when eaten is consistent with the Chinese feeling about food. For to the Chinese, eating is a pleasurable pastime, not just a necessity. There are also a wide variety of rice and noodle dishes and Chinese sweets that can be served as dim sum, for leisurely consumption between meals or at odd moments.

Until recently there were only a few teahouses in the United States, usually serving a limited menu only on weekends. But as more Chinese have moved here, and more Americans have discovered the pleasures of dim sum, these teahouses have begun to flourish in American Chinatowns. Most are open from early morning to mid-afternoon, serving a wide variety of teas as the sole beverage. Since this is the only type of Chinese restaurant where you can choose your tea, Cantonese people use the term "yam cha," meaning "drink tea," whenever they decide to go to a teahouse. But no one ever goes there just to drink tea!

All the mouth-watering delicacies, handmade and freshly cooked every day, are carried out piping hot on trays or pushed on carts by waiters or waitresses who circulate around the customers' tables. The waitresses chant their wares in Cantonese, a Southern Chinese dialect. And, since there usually is no menu, you point to the dish of your choice as the waitresses pass by with the dim sum. The food is then brought to your table, usually three or four bite-sized pieces to a small plate. The noodle and rice dishes are not circulated by the waiter or waitress, so they have to be ordered. They come on large plates, and are commonly shared among a group of diners. However, each order by itself makes a well-balanced, substantial meal for one person.

The idea in the teahouses is to enjoy the food at your own pace. You don't need to take everything you see on first sight; the dim sum will be recirculated and there will be other varieties coming. You will want to pace yourself, sipping tea and nibbling, as the Chinese do, so as not to fill up with food too quickly.

These teahouses are usually crowded and noisy on weekends, and you may even find yourself sharing a table with strangers. But don't be intimidated by the mob. To the Chinese, a teahouse is a place for a family outing, a place to meet friends and have breakfast, snacks or lunch. You'll see office workers, young lovers, business associates or families of three or four generations, complete with children and babies, chatting and drinking tea. Yet no matter how busy or crowded, no one ever hurries you to leave. Stay as long as you like and, when you are finished, gesture for the bill. The waiter or waitress will count the number of dishes, then tabulate the cost—which is usually quite inexpensive. And, as you will see, you need not know a word of Chinese.

Enjoying Teahouse Food in American Homes

Although an increasing number of Americans have discovered Chinese teahouses, few have tried to make these Chinese pastries and dumplings at home. Their preparation may seem complex if you don't know the technique, but there are just four basic and logical steps:
1. Making the filling.
2. Making the wrapper (for some recipes in this book, you can buy ready-made wrappers at Oriental food stores or at some American supermarkets).
3. Shaping the dim sum.
4. Cooking the finished dim sum.

Americans have long taken for granted such modern household conveniences as running water, the refrigerator, the freezer and the modern stove that provides instant heat with the flick of a knob. But in fact, these things are still not available in many areas of mainland China today: the majority of Chinese people still use charcoal for cooking. One of my most vivid recollections from my recent China trip is the amount of time required to produce the exact heat needed for good Chinese cooking over a charcoal fire. Anyone who knows a few fundamentals will agree that Chinese cooking is easier in a modern American kitchen.

Since home refrigeration is still unknown in large parts of China, dim sum have to be prepared and served there on the same day. But in America, where this problem does not exist, each of the four preparation steps can be completed at a different time. For instance, you can make the filling a few days ahead and refrigerate it, make the wrappers at a later date, and if some wrappers are available ready-made, keep them in the freezer, defrosting them just before shaping. Shaped dim sum can be refrigerated or frozen, and if some are cooked ahead, just reheat them before serving.

Finding special Chinese ingredients, for dim sum and other dishes, is no longer a problem in America. Many American supermarkets now sell Chinese staples, and Oriental food stores are appearing even in small American towns and suburbs. And now there are excellent, reliable mail-order houses supplying sources of Chinese ingredients or cooking equipment.

Actually, many dim sum can be eaten as a whole meal, served alone when made in sufficient quantity or as excellent hors d'oeuvres. They can be used as a pace setter for a formal meal or a main feature at cocktail parties. You need only master one or two kinds to make entertaining a little special, and the advanced preparation gives you the time and peace of mind to enjoy your own party.

You might plan a larger dim sum party by using many more kinds of dim sum and selecting different fillings and cooking methods. But decide on what you can handle with ease, using equipment on hand, and choosing food that can be prepared ahead. Do as much advance preparation as possible before the party. Serve the dim sum buffet style, or one food at a time.

The noodle and rice dishes also make wonderful, economical everyday family meals for hearty eaters but are just as adaptable for small families or singles. They can be cooked in small quantities and then there will be no leftovers.

Whether you are making a complete Chinese meal, or incorporating these dishes with your Western food, whether you are looking for time-saving ideas for everyday meals or intriguing cook-ahead hors d'oeuvres, you can be sure to find something to suit your taste in this book of dim sum cooking.

Helpful Hints

1. An asterisk (*), when appearing after a step in the recipe, indicates that the recipe can be prepared or cooked in advance through that particular step. When * appears after the last cooking step, it means the entire dish can be cooked ahead. For storing and rewarming information, see Notes in each recipe.

2. For those who have a food processor, there is a section on techniques for using it. For those who do not have one, there is a section on hand-cutting techniques.

3. Unless the recipe specifies to remove ingredients, they should remain in the food processor while others are being added.

4. Unless indicated, it is not necessary to wash the beaker (workbowl) of the food processor when progressing from one ingredient to the next in the same recipe.

5. Within recipes, preparations such as "mince" and "chop finely" are indicated along with the ingredients; when the food processor is used, such preparations are given as part of the instruction section.

6. Chinese cooking utensils are not necessary. All the recipes use "wok" in general terms only; a heavy skillet can be substituted. To use the wok on an electric burner, read the section on the wok (page 18).

7. To avoid last-minute confusion when making stir-fried dishes, it is a good practice to have all the ingredients ready and arranged near the stove in the order they will be added to the wok. I have included a "Have Ready Before Cooking" section for these recipes to help you organize your cooking. For the best results, make sure the meat is totally defrosted before stir frying.

8. Soy sauce varies in color and taste from brand to brand. For uniform results, and unless otherwise specified, recipes in this book were tested with Kikkoman soy sauce, an all-purpose soy sauce widely available in supermarkets. (For more information on soy sauce, see page 25.)

9. Chicken broth varies in color and saltiness from brand to brand. For uniform results, all the recipes in this book were tested with College Inn brand.

10. A kitchen scale is very useful. To get good results with the recipes, accurate measurement of ingredients is important.

11. Cooking oil can be corn oil, peanut oil or any vegetable oil except olive oil.

12. In making dough, the proportions of flour and liquid may vary with the weather and the kind of flour used. Use the amount of liquid specified in the recipe as a guideline, adding more or less to get the necessary consistency.

Equipment and Utensils

THE FOOD PROCESSOR

This versatile machine has revolutionized modern kitchens. It is now a standard appliance for millions of American families, and many wonder what they ever did without it. One of its greatest assets is its speed, allowing more to be accomplished in less time.

Although originally intended for French cooking, the machine is equally useful in the preparation of Chinese food. In just seconds, it chops, minces, purees, slices, shreds, mixes and kneads.

The processor will slice partially frozen meat and chicken to uniform slices, and to just the right size and thickness for stir-fried dishes. It chops meat to coarse, medium and fine textures close to those achieved by the hand chopping traditionally done by Chinese cooks. For those concerned with weight and cholesterol levels, the biggest advantage of using a food processor is that it enables them to control the exact amount of fat that goes into the chopped meat.

General Tips

Always wait until the disk or the blade has stopped spinning before removing the cover of the beaker.

To minimize the washing of the beaker, work from dry to wet ingredients. Recipes in this book are designed in such order.

To simplify cleaning, wash processor parts immediately after using, so food will not dry on the surface.

To Slice Vegetables

(medium ⅛-inch or fine 1/12-inch slicing disk) Use the pusher as a guide to the length and width of foods to be sliced. For uniform slices, cut off the flat end of the vegetable, and cut the vegetable to a length shorter than the feed tube. Place the cut vegetable in the feed tube with the flat side down.

For thin, round vegetables like carrots and celery, wedge them tightly in the feed tube, keeping them upright.

For wide, round vegetables like cucumbers or zucchini, place the vegetable on the right side of the feed tube with the feed tube at the front of the beaker. This will keep it upright.

Use light pressure for soft food, firm pressure for harder food.

To Prepare Raw Meat and Chicken for Slicing

To prepare meat, use the pusher of the processor as a guide, and cut the meat into pieces about 2 inches wide by 3½ inches long that will fit the feed tube. Soft meat at room temperature does not slice well, so partially freeze meat until it is firm to the touch but can be pierced through with a sharp, pointed knife. (Do not attempt to slice it if the knife cannot go through.)

To prepare chicken, start with boneless, skinless breasts. Cut them down the middle to separate the two half breasts. Remove any hard membrane and fat. Detach the small layer underneath the large piece and remove its white tendon. Lay the two large and two small pieces from a whole breast side by side. Soft chicken at room temperature does not slice well, so partially freeze the pieces on a flat surface without overlapping until they are hard to the touch but can be pierced through with a sharp, pointed knife. (Do not attempt to slice if the knife cannot go through.) Cut parts in half across the grain to fit the length of the feed tube for slicing.

When preparing meat and chicken for slicing, bear in mind that the pieces will be placed flatside down in the feed tube with the grain of the muscle running perpendicular to the slicing disk.

To Slice Raw Meat and Chicken
(medium slicing disk—⅛ inch)
A machine with a high horsepower will slice meat and chicken easily; others may not do as well, so it is best to check the instruction manual of your machine.

To get uniform slices, wedge partially frozen meat or chicken snugly in the feed tube, keeping pieces upright, and with the grain of the muscle running perpendicular to the slicing disk. Use firm, steady pressure on the pusher. Expect the machine to make more noise than when slicing vegetables.

To Freeze Meat and Chicken for Future Use
It is very handy to have meat and chicken on hand in the freezer. With meat, freeze 2-inch-wide pieces flat in a baking pan, then store in a well-sealed plastic bag in the freezer. With chicken, wrap the two large and two small pieces from a whole breast in plastic wrap, being

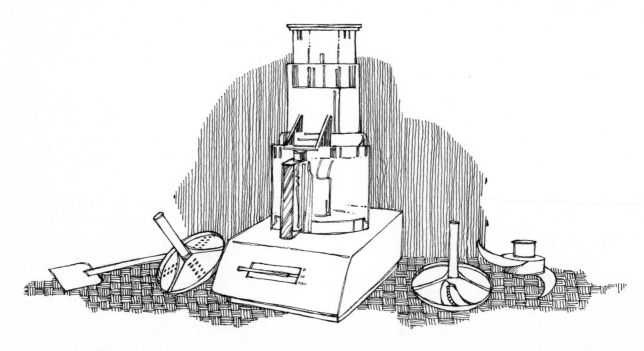

careful not to overlap the pieces. Freeze on a flat surface. If you are freezing several breasts, wrap each breast individually, then stack packages one on top of the other and place in a well-sealed plastic bag. Freeze on a flat surface.

A microwave oven will partially defrost three-quarters of a pound of meat in about a minute on "high" setting, and will partially defrost a chicken breast in about 30 seconds on "high" setting.

To Chop and Mince Food (steel blade)
One of the processor's most useful functions for Chinese cooking is chopping food, especially meat. The processor can make the exact kind of chopped meat you want—coarsely or finely chopped, lean, medium or fat, with the same texture you would get from hand chopping.

Cut food into cubes no larger than 1 inch; the more uniform the cubes, the more uniform your results. Use on/off turns (or press pulse button on new processor). This means a quick twist in turning the machine on, then turning it off rapidly. The on/off technique makes it possible to achieve an even chop without danger of overprocessing. The machine works so fast that the contents must be checked very frequently to see if the desired results have been achieved. If food is overprocessed you can end up with a puree.

Whether food is coarsely or finely chopped is regulated by the number of on/off turns or pulses with some of the newer food processors ("on/off turns" will be used in the recipes in this book), and by the total processing time.

You should chop no more than two cups of vegetables at one time, and no more than one cup (about a half pound) of meat at one time if coarsely chopped meat is desired. However, you can chop two cups at one time if the meat is to be finely minced. You can chop up to three cups of meat at once in a processor with a larger beaker (workbowl). Remove coarse membranes and gristles before or after processing.

To Freeze Meat Cubes for Future Use
Since many recipes in this book call for chopped meat, it is very handy to keep some meat cubes in the freezer. Cut boneless pork or beef into 1-inch cubes and freeze individually first, then combine and store them in a plastic bag for future use.

A machine with high horsepower can chop partially frozen meat cubes very well. A microwave oven will partially defrost one pound of meat cubes in a minute on "high" setting.

To Make Pastry Dough (steel blade)
Process pastry dough with the steel blade. Recipes in the book are based on the original smaller-sized beaker (workbowl). If you have a larger processor, you may use more flour in each batch. Check the instruction book of your processor for its maximum capacity.

To Make Yeast Dough
(short plastic dough blade or steel blade)
The short plastic dough blade is designed especially for mixing and kneading yeast bread dough. It prevents the machine from overheating while the dough is being kneaded. However, not all machines have this accessory, in which case you can use the steel blade. Just don't let the machine run as long if it begins to overheat. A quick kneading by hand should finish the job.

Recipes in this book are based on the original smaller-sized beaker (workbowl). If you have a larger processor, you may use more flour in each batch. Check the instruction book of your processor for its maximum capacity.

WOK
The wok's curved bottom allows for the best use of even the smallest amount of oil; it can therefore cook a very small amount of food efficiently. Its large surface and spherical shape also allow ingredients to be stirred vigorously without

spilling. The wok is the most versatile and economical cooking utensil ever invented.

Woks made of iron distribute heat more evenly and cook better than stainless steel and aluminum woks. A 14-inch wok is the most practical size for home use.

To season a new wok, wash it with detergent and hot water to remove any industrial grease, then dry it thoroughly. Heat the wok over medium heat. With a paper towel, spread a thin layer of cooking oil over the entire inside surface. Heat one to two minutes or until the wok is very hot, then rinse it with hot water. Dry the wok thoroughly over heat, and spread another thin layer of cooking oil over the surface. Heat again, and repeat the whole process one or more times. The wok is now ready to be used.

After each cooking, while the wok is still hot, use a hard or bamboo brush to scrub it clean with hot water or mild soap; hard detergent will remove the seasoning. Dry thoroughly after each washing. To prevent it from rusting, oil occasionally after washing and drying when the wok is still new.

The wok usually comes in a set with a large dome-shaped cover and a ring. The ring is useful for stabilizing the wok when it is used for steaming or deep-frying.

To use on an electric burner, heat the wok directly on electric coils until the coils are red and the wok is very hot, then add the oil and heat to the desired temperature before adding ingredients. If the heat is too high or the food starts to burn, remove the wok from the heat for a short time, or cook on a second burner at medium heat, moving the wok back and forth to get the correct heat.

If you do not have a wok, a heavy skillet can be used instead.

LONG-HANDLED SPATULA
This is longer than the western spatula, and is designed for use with the wok for easy stirring. A Western spatula can be substituted.

WIRE STRAINER
This strainer with bamboo handle comes in all sizes, and is used for draining fried or blanched foods. A slotted spoon can be used instead.

CLEAVER

This comes in different sizes and weights and is made of stainless steel or carbon steel. The latter can be sharpened more easily to a finer edge and is better for cutting. However, it will rust, so it should be cleaned and dried shortly after using.

Sharpen the cleaver frequently. A sharp cleaver makes cutting easier, and is actually a safer knife.

A good, sharp, Western knife can be used instead of a cleaver.

Hand-Cutting Techniques

Cutting is a very important part of preparation in Chinese cooking. Since only chopsticks are used to eat the food, all the cutting is usually done beforehand in the kitchen.

A good stable cutting board and a sharp cleaver or knife are essential. Firmly grasp the handle and part of the blade of the cleaver with your writing hand. Use your other hand to hold and press the food in place on the cutting board. The fingertips of this hand should be bent back a little and, to protect them, the first joints should be in contact with the side of the cleaver. To ensure safety, do not lift the blade of the cleaver above the level of the joints. Use a forward and downward press to cut food, not a back-and-forth sawing motion. In order to ensure even cooking and a pleasing appearance, it is important to cut the food uniformly.

To Slice

Meat and chicken are much easier to slice when partially frozen. They should be sliced across the grain to achieve tenderness. Unless specified in the recipe, cut into about ¾-inch-wide by 1½- to 2-inch-long by ⅛-inch-thick slices.

To Shred

To get julienne strips, first cut the food into ⅛-inch-thick by 2-inch-long slices, then stack several slices and cut into ⅛-inch-wide shreds about the size of matchsticks.

To Cube

Cut ingredients into 1-inch-thick strips, then cut strips into 1-inch cubes.

To Dice

Cut ingredients into ¼-inch or ½-inch-thick slices, then into ¼-inch or ½-inch-wide strips. Gather the strips together, and cut them across into ¼-inch or ½-inch cubes.

To Mince

First cut the food into small dice, then chop with quick motions of the cleaver. Keep the tip of the cleaver on the cutting surface and pivot the blade while cutting the ingredients continuously with a rocking motion. Coarsely mince to the size of rice or a quarter of a pea, or finely mince to the size of a sesame seed.

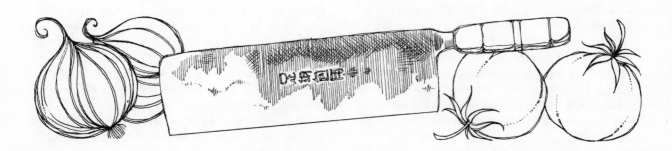

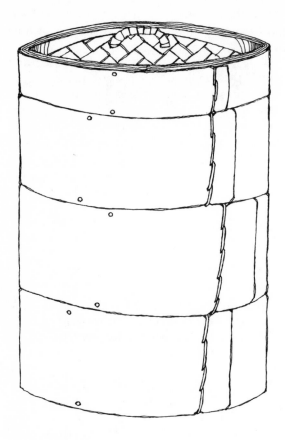

To improvise with utensils in your kitchen, use a large pot or a roaster. The pot has to be at least 1 inch larger in diameter than the bowl in which the food is placed, and it should be large enough to contain enough water and provide sufficient space for the hot steam to circulate around the food. The food has to be suspended above the boiling water, so the water does not bubble over it. For this you can use a 2-inch-tall can with both ends removed or 2 cans with the ends removed in a roaster. Place a rack on top of the can or cans. Fill water to 1 inch below the rack and bring it to a boil, then place the food on the rack to steam. Cover the pot with a well-fitted cover. A steady volume of steam should be maintained throughout the steaming, so check occasionally to see if you need to add more hot water to the pot.

CHOPSTICKS

These are indispensable in Chinese kitchens, for they are used for cooking as well as eating.

MICROWAVE OVEN

A microwave oven will save a lot of time in defrosting ingredients and heating precooked foods. Since it works so fast, when in doubt it is better to undercook or underdefrost the food. Some food will not be good if overheated by microwave oven. Several convenient applications of a microwave oven are given below.

(The timing below is a guideline for the oven at a "high" setting. It may vary somewhat with different ovens. In general, heating time increases in proportion to the amount of food being heated. Use utensils that are recommended for the microwave oven.)

• It partially defrosts one pound of meat or chicken for slicing or chopping in about one minute.

• It is excellent for rewarming precooked rice and noodles. Heat them directly in a covered

STEAMER

The traditional bamboo steamer is ingeniously designed. It comes in many different sizes and in several layers, with each layer fitting on top of the other, so several dishes can be cooked at the same time on the same burner, saving both fuel and cooking space. To steam, the stacked layers are set onto a wok containing boiling water.

A Western steamer can be substituted. There are also inexpensive aluminum perforated steaming trays designed to fit right into the wok, and modern aluminum steamers that come in two layers with a pot underneath to hold the boiling water.

serving bowl. A piece of plastic wrap works well as a cover.

 1 cup cold boiled rice: heat about
  1 minute
 2 cups cold boiled rice: heat about
  2 minutes
 2 cups frozen boiled rice: heat about
  4 minutes
 2 cups cold boiled noodles: heat about
  1 minute

• It is the best way to reheat leftover stir-fried dishes. Heat them uncovered, stirring once during heating.

• It is perfect for rewarming fried rice and many of the noodle dishes in this book.

• It defrosts and warms frozen steamed and baked buns wrapped in plastic wrap. Timing is very important here, for overheating will dry out the bread. Since microwave ovens differ, experiment with yours to find out the right time.

Chinese Ingredients

BAMBOO SHOOTS 筍

Bamboo shoots grow during different seasons. The winter ones are the best tasting and are also the most expensive. Fresh ones are hard to obtain outside China, but canned ones are widely available.

Once opened, they can be stored in a bottle of fresh water and kept in the refrigerator. If you change the water every two or three days, they will keep for a few weeks.

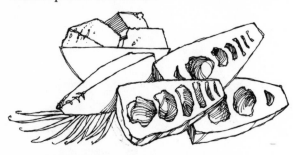

BEAN CURD, FRESH 豆腐

Also known as Tofu, bean curd comes in ¾-by-3-by-3-inch individual pieces, or in 1-pound blocks sealed in plastic containers. Both hard and soft bean curd are now available in many American supermarkets. This rather bland-tasting, ivory-colored, custard-like product is made from soy bean milk.

Unopened bean curd can be kept in the refrigerator for one to two weeks. Once opened, it should be kept covered with fresh water in the refrigerator. Changing water every day may keep it unspoiled for a week.

BEAN SPROUTS 綠豆芽

Fresh bean sprouts are now available in most supermarkets. They should be plump and white, not brownish. Canned ones are not good for recipes in this book.

If they are kept very dry, they can stay fresh in a tightly sealed container for two or three days; otherwise, keep them in fresh water, and change the water every day.

BOK CHOY 白菜

This has white stems with green leaves and tastes most like Swiss chard. Choose the smaller ones, for they are more tender. Many American supermarkets now sell this vegetable.

If kept free from moisture, and wrapped first in a brown paper bag, then in a well-sealed plastic bag, bok choy will last for a week.

BROWN BEAN SAUCE 原晒豉

This salty, thick, brownish sauce is made from fermented soy beans. It is available in cans or jars.

If it is from a can, once opened it should be transferred to a covered jar. It will keep under refrigeration for many months.

CELERY CABBAGE 黄芽白菜

There are two kinds. Chinese groceries sell only the fatter and shorter ones, labeled Nappa cabbage in some American supermarkets. These are more tender than the long-headed, thinner variety.

Keep celery cabbage free from moisture in a plastic bag. It will keep in the refrigerator for over two weeks.

HOT CHILI OIL 辣油

This is available in Chinese grocery stores. The commercial product is orange in color. Just a small amount is needed to spice up the food. You can use Tabasco as a substitute.

To make chili oil: in a small pot, heat ½ cup cooking oil over medium heat until it just starts to smoke. Remove pot from heat and wait for about 1 minute. Add 20 hot dry peppers to warm oil, then fry until peppers turn dark brown. If an orange color is desired, stir in 1 teaspoon paprika. Remove from heat and cover the pot. Line funnel with paper towel, and filter the oil after cooling.

HOT DRY RED PEPPERS 辣椒

These are about 1 to 2 inches long and are available in Chinese or Italian grocery stores. You can substitute crushed red pepper flakes.

They will keep indefinitely in a dry container at room temperature.

EGG ROLL WRAPPERS 廣東春卷皮

(*see Spring Roll Wrappers*)

These 8-inch squares are machine made from wheat flour, egg and water, and are packed in 1- to 2-pound packages. To make your own, see the recipe in this book.

Stored in a well-sealed plastic bag, they will keep in the refrigerator for three or four days, and in the freezer for two to three months.

GINGER, FRESH 薑

Now available in most American supermarkets, this beige-colored root is indispensable in Chinese cooking. Ginger powder should not be used as a substitute.

It will keep in the refrigerator for many months if peeled, covered with dry sherry and stored in a jar.

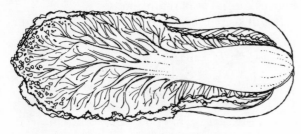

MUSHROOMS, DRY CHINESE 冬菇

Brownish black in color, these have a lovely flavor and texture. They must be soaked in boiling water until softened, and the hard stem should be cut off before using.

They will keep indefinitely in a dry container in the refrigerator.

NOODLES, FRESH EGG 蛋麵

These are sold fresh in 1-pound bags in the refrigerator sections of Chinese food stores. Cooking time depends on the thickness, which varies from manufacturer to manufacturer. To make your own, see page 69. Chinese dry noodles, American or Italian homemade fresh or packaged dry noodles, and spaghetti can be used as substitutes.

Fresh egg noodles will keep in the refrigerator for two to three days and in the freezer for many months. Defrosting is not necessary before boiling the noodles.

NOODLES, FRESH RICE (*Sha Ho Fun*) 沙河粉

Made from regular rice powder, these are available in some noodle or bean curd stores in Chinatowns.

They will keep in the refrigerator for two days, and in the freezer for several months.

NOODLES, DRY RICE (*Rice sticks*) 米粉

Made from regular rice flour, these are sold in 1-pound packages in Chinese food stores. Their thickness varies with different brands. Parboiling is not necessary; just soak noodles in warm water for a short period until soft. Dried ones can be deep-fried to be used as garnish.

They will keep indefinitely in dry forms at room temperature.

ORANGE PEEL, DRIED 陳皮

A brownish-colored dried peel, this adds an orange flavor to food.

It will keep indefinitely in a jar at room temperature.

OYSTER-FLAVORED SAUCE 蠔油

A thick brownish sauce made from oyster extract, this has a rich and subtle taste and enhances the flavor of many foods.

It will keep indefinitely at room temperature.

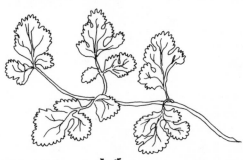

PARSLEY, CHINESE 香菜

Also known as cilantro or coriander, this looks somewhat like flat Italian parsley but has a very strong and distinct flavor and aroma. Available in Chinese, Spanish and Indian food stores, it is used for seasoning or as a garnish.

Place roots and stems in a jar filled with water, then cover the leaves with a plastic bag. It will keep in the refrigerator for several weeks.

RED BEAN PASTE 豆沙

Made from puree of red bean and sugar, this is used as a filling in Chinese sweets. It can be homemade or purchased canned.

RICE, GLUTINOUS 糯米

Also known as sweet rice or sticky rice, this is an opaque, white, short rice that becomes sticky when cooked.

Store in a dry place as you would regular rice.

RICE WINE 黄酒

A Chinese wine made from fermented rice, this is usually served warm. Lower grade ones are used in cooking, but you can substitute dry sherry. Some American liquor stores carry rice wines; they are always available in liquor stores in Chinatowns.

SAUSAGE, CHINESE 臘腸

About 5 to 6 inches long, the reddish-colored Chinese sausages are made with pork and have a savory, sweetish flavor. The brownish ones are made with duck liver. Both should be steamed for 15 minutes or cooked before eating.

They will keep in the refrigerator for several weeks.

SESAME OIL 麻油

Made from roasted sesame seeds, this dark golden oil has a rich nutty flavor and is much more aromatic than the light-colored sesame oil sold in the health food stores, which should not be used as a substitute. Both Chinese and Japanese brands are good.

It will keep for a few months at room temperature.

SHRIMP, DRIED 蝦米

These are very salty, and can be softened by soaking in boiling water.

They will keep indefinitely in a tightly sealed container in the refrigerator.

SOY SAUCE 醬油

Chinese soy sauce comes in light and dark (or thin and black). Light soy sauce is actually saltier than the dark sauce, which has a slightly sweet caramel taste. In this cookbook, unless specified, Kikkoman soy sauce, the naturally brewed all-purpose Japanese soy sauce, is used in all recipes. It is available in American supermarkets; large bottles and ½ to 1-gallon cans are available in Chinese grocery stores. Soy sauce differs in taste from brand to brand, so the flavor of the dish will vary depending upon the soy sauce used.

Soy sauce will keep for a long time at room temperature.

SPRING ROLL WRAPPERS 春卷皮

These are not the same as Cantonese egg roll wrappers and are thinner, more delicate and crisper after frying than Cantonese egg roll wrappers. Handmade ones are 8-inch rounds; machine-made ones are squares. Both are sold in sealed plastic bags; unfortunately, some are confusingly labeled "egg roll skins," so check with the store clerks to make sure.

They will keep in the refrigerator for two to three days, and in the freezer for two to three months. The wrappers dry out easily and are then difficult to handle, so wrap them in another well-sealed plastic bag before storing.

STAR ANISE 八角

Shaped like an eight-pointed star, this is a brownish, hard, dry spice about 1 inch in size with a strong licorice flavor.

It will keep indefinitely at room temperature.

SZECHUAN PEPPERCORNS 花椒

Reddish-brown with opened husks, these are not really hot but have a distinct aroma.

They will keep indefinitely in a closed container at room temperature.

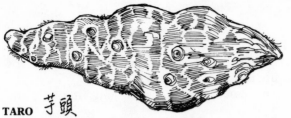

TARO 芋頭

This is the root of a tropical plant; it is starchy like a potato and has dusty rough brownish skin. Some large ones weigh over 2 pounds. They are available year-round in Chinatowns.

Fresh ones can be kept at room temperature for a few days. Cooked ones can be kept in the freezer for many months.

VINEGAR, CHINESE RED 大紅浙醋

Milder than Western vinegar, it has a delicate flavor and makes a delicious dip for spring rolls and dumplings.

It will keep for a long time at room temperature.

WATER CHESTNUTS 荸薺

Fresh water chestnuts (canned ones are available in American supermarkets) are sweet and crunchy, but be sure to peel off the skin before using.

Fresh water chestnuts are quite perishable. But you can refrigerate canned water chestnuts, once opened, covered with fresh water in a jar, if you change the water every other day. In this way, they will keep for more than two weeks.

WHEAT STARCH 澄麵粉

This flour, sold in 1-pound bags, has had its gluten portion removed. It is used as wrappers for delicate dumplings, but the dough has no elasticity and must be carefully handled.

Store wheat starch the same as flour.

WONTON WRAPPERS 餛飩皮

Machine-made wonton wrappers of wheat flour, egg and water come in various thicknesses and are sold in 1-pound packages. You'll have to ask store clerks for the correct thickness since there is no indication on the wrapper. See the recipe in this book (on page 69) to make your own wrappers.

To prevent drying of wonton wrappers, keep them in a well-sealed plastic bag. They can be refrigerated for two to three days, or frozen for three to four months. You may want to divide them into smaller packages before freezing.

DIM SUM

點 心

Deep-Fried Foods

Deep-frying is a universal cooking method in which a large quantity of oil is brought to a high temperature. Food is then cooked in the hot oil until it is done, usually crispy and golden outside.

In deep-frying, the oil must be deep enough so that the food will float in it. A wok with its round bottom has the benefit of using less oil to reach the desired depth, so it works very well as a deep-fryer, provided you have a gas burner. Be sure to have a ring underneath to prevent the hot oil from spilling. The wok does not work as well on an electric burner, for once the food is added to the oil, the oil temperature usually drops since the electric coil loses too much heat on the side—it takes too long to get the oil back to the required temperature again. On an electric burner it is more practical to fry in a flat-bottomed pot.

To test the temperature of the oil, drop a small piece of bread into it. If it turns golden brown in one minute, the oil temperature is about 350 degrees. If it browns in 40 seconds, the temperature is about 375 degrees. If you don't have a piece of bread, dip a dry bamboo chopstick into the oil. When lots of bubbles gather around the chopstick, the oil is ready for frying. A deep-frying or candy thermometer, an electric wok or a deep-fryer with a temperature control help maintain the correct temperature while frying.

Oil temperature is important. If the oil is not hot enough, the food will absorb too much of it and become greasy; if the oil is too hot, the food will brown too quickly outside but remain uncooked inside. To help maintain the correct temperature, do not cook too many pieces of food at one time.

Cooking time depends on the type, size and amount of food being fried and the efficiency of your heat. Drop or slide food gently into the hot oil to prevent splattering.

Leftover oil from frying can be reused. Strain and keep it in a covered bottle in the refrigerator. Oil used for seafood should be reused only with seafood, because other foods cooked in it take on a seafood flavor. To refresh the used oil, add two slices of fresh ginger while heating the oil and discard ginger when golden brown. Once the oil becomes heavy and dark, it should be thrown out.

Shrimp Rolls

Wonderful as finger food, these crisp and delicate shrimp rolls are very easy to make. Although best when freshly fried, shrimp rolls are still delicious if made far in advance, then refried or reheated in the oven just before serving. This is also an economical recipe for using shrimp: as you will see, half a pound of it goes a long way.

SHRIMP MIXTURE:
½ pound shrimp with shells (20 to 30 count per pound)
1 cube fresh ginger, ½ inch
1 large scallion (white top only)
4 medium-size water chestnuts
1½ teaspoons cornstarch
1 teaspoon salt or to taste
½ teaspoon sugar
2 teaspoons dry sherry
1 egg white
2 teaspoons sesame oil (optional)

8 Shanghai spring roll skins (use square ones; see Variation for substitute)
1 egg yolk, slightly beaten
Cooking oil for deep frying

PREPARATION: Shell, devein and wash the shrimp. Then drain and pat dry with paper towels.

With steel blade in place, mince ginger and scallion top. Then add water chestnuts and chop with 2 quick on/off turns. Add shrimp and remaining ingredients for shrimp mixture. Process with on/off turns until shrimp is finely minced.*

(Without a food processor, mince ingredients by hand; combine the shrimp mixture and mix thoroughly in a bowl.*)

SHAPING: Cut each spring roll skin into 4 squares, about 3½-inches each. Take 1 square and place 1 rounded teaspoon of shrimp mixture in the middle of 1 side, leaving about 1 inch from each end of the filling. Roll the wrapper like a cigarette. Seal the edges with slightly beaten egg yolk. Repeat with the other squares.*

COOKING: Heat the oil to 350 degrees for deep-frying. Fry shrimp rolls about 2 minutes, until golden and crisp. Fry in several batches; do not overcrowd. Drain on paper towels. Keep them warm in a low oven while the others are being fried. Serve hot.*

NOTE: Uncooked rolls can be made ½ to 1 day ahead and kept in the refrigerator. Cover well with plastic wrap. Cooked rolls can be kept in the refrigerator for 2 days, in the freezer for several weeks. Defrosting is not necessary; just reheat in a preheated 350-degree oven on a rack over a baking pan for 20 minutes, or until heated through and crispy. Turn once during heating. Frozen rolls may take longer.

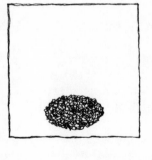

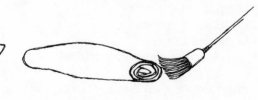

VARIATION: You can substitute the more readily available egg roll or thin wonton wrappers for Shanghai spring roll wrappers, but neither gives exactly the same appearance or crispness. You do not have to cut the wonton wrappers.

If you cannot find any of these wrappers, you can use very thin white bread. With a knife, trim crust from 16 pieces of fresh bread. Then with a rolling pin, roll and press the bread as thinly as possible. Cut each piece in half, and use each half as a wrapper. This will not have the same texture as authentic wrappers, but it is also delicious.

Fried Shrimp Sandwiches

Makes 48

Our Shanghai cook always used to make shrimp toast in sandwich style. Though we ate it as one of the several dishes for the main meal, it is also delicious served as an hors d'oeuvre and can be made ahead. The fresher the shrimp, the better the taste.

The bread should be made at least two days ahead, although it can be quick-dried if advance preparation is not possible (see note).

24 slices very thin white bread (preferably ¼ inch thick)

SHRIMP MIXTURE:
1 pound shrimp with shells (20 to 30 count per pound)
2 cubes fresh ginger, ½ inch each
3 scallions (white tops only)
4 ounces water chestnuts
1 tablespoon cornstarch
2 teaspoons salt, or to taste
1 teaspoon sugar
1 tablespoon dry sherry
1 large egg
1 tablespoon sesame oil (optional)

1 quart cooking oil for deep-frying

PREPARATION: Prepare bread at least 2 days ahead. (Or for quick drying of bread, see note.) Trim off crusts with a knife, then cut each slice into 4 triangles. Spread triangles out and let dry in air for 2 days or longer. Dried bread can be kept for many weeks.

Shell, devein and wash the shrimp. Then drain and pat dry with paper towels.

With steel blade in place, mince ginger and scallion tops. Then add water chestnuts and chop with 2 quick on/off turns. Add shrimp and remaining ingredients for shrimp mixture. Process with quick on/off turns until shrimp is finely minced.

(Without food processor, mince ingredients by hand, then combine and mix the shrimp mixture thoroughly in a bowl.)

Spread each triangle with 1 heaping teaspoon of shrimp mixture, then cover with another triangle to make small sandwiches.*

COOKING: Heat oil for deep-frying to 350 degrees. Fry sandwiches in batches until both sides are golden and crisp. Do not overcrowd. Drain on paper towels and serve hot.*

NOTE: Uncooked sandwiches can be kept in the refrigerator about ½ day, covered with plastic wrap. Cooked sandwiches can be kept in the refrigerator for 2 or 3 days, in the freezer for about 2 months. It is not necessary to defrost them, just reheat in a preheated, 350-degree oven on a rack over a baking pan for 20 minutes, or until heated through and crisp. Turn once during heating.

You can speed up drying of the bread by heating slices on a rack in a 200-degree oven for about 1 hour. Or in a microwave oven, line the oven with double layers of paper towels, then place 24 triangles on the towels. Heat on "Bake" or a low setting for 3 minutes. Time may vary somewhat depending on your microwave oven. Repeat with the other 24 triangles.

Miniature Pear-Shaped Dumplings

Pan Hsi, the most famous dim sum restaurant in China, is situated in Canton, where teahouses originated. It is a large complex that seats 3,000 and has more than 20 chefs who specialize in dim sum. The restaurant is known not only for its variety of dim sum, but also for the enchanting shapes and artful presentations of its food.

Pear-shaped dumplings are one such creation of the Pan Hsi chefs. Interestingly seasoned with curry flavor, these dumplings are shaped like miniature pears. They will certainly delight your company as well as your family, and they are wonderful hors d'oeuvres. What's more, these dumplings are easy to make, do not require exotic ingredients and can be prepared many days ahead.

CURRY FILLING *(Makes 1¼ cups; use ¾ cup for this recipe)*

8 shallots (about ⅓ cup chopped, or use equivalent amount of onion)
5 large water chestnuts (about ¼ cup chopped)

PORK MIXTURE:
6 ounces boneless pork in 1-inch cubes, or ground pork without processor
1 teaspoon cornstarch
2 teaspoons dry sherry
2 teaspoons soy sauce

2 tablespoons cooking oil
2 teaspoons curry powder or to taste

SAUCE MIXTURE:
½ teaspoon salt or to taste
1 teaspoon sugar or to taste
1 tablespoon dry sherry
1 tablespoon soy sauce

1 teaspoon cornstarch mixed with 2 teaspoons water

PREPARATION OF FILLING: With steel blade in place, chop shallots, then remove from beaker. Then chop water chestnuts and remove from beaker. Put pork mixture in the beaker and process with on/off turns until pork is minced.*

(Without food processor, chop shallots and water chestnuts by hand. Mix ground pork and remaining pork mixture ingredients in large bowl.*)

COOKING OF FILLING: Heat the wok, then heat 2 tablespoons oil. Cook shallots on medium heat for about 1 minute. Add curry powder, and cook for 30 seconds. Do not burn the powder. If it gets too dry, add a little more oil. Add pork mixture, and stir-fry until pork almost loses its pink color. Add water chestnuts and sauce mixture, stirring to mix. Add cornstarch mixture, and cook until sauce is thickened.*

NOTE: Filling can be made ahead and will keep in the refrigerator for 1 week.

POTATO DOUGH: *(Makes 2 cups)*

1 pound potatoes, washed with skins on
3 tablespoons cornstarch
2 tablespoons vegetable shortening or lard
1 teaspoon salt
1 teaspoon sugar
½ teaspoon curry powder or to taste
Dash ground black pepper

¼ cup unseasoned breadcrumbs
1 small carrot, cut into 32 1-inch-long, match-sized sticks
Cooking oil for deep-frying

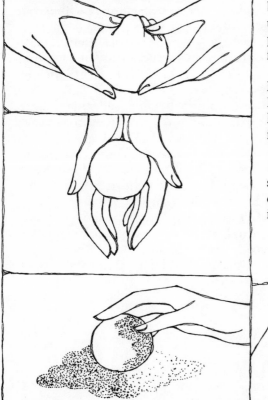

PREPARATION: Cook potatoes with skins on in boiling water for 40 minutes, or until soft when tested with a fork. Drain in a colander, and let cool. Peel potatoes, then cut into 1-inch cubes.

With steel blade in place, process potato with a few on/off turns until coarsely chopped. Add remaining ingredients for potato dough. Process just until a smooth dough is formed, and all the ingredients are mixed.*

(Without food processor, mash potato with a fork or a potato ricer. Add remaining ingredients for potato dough, and beat with an electric mixer until the ingredients are well mixed and the dough is smooth like thick mashed potatoes.*)

SHAPING: Flatten 1 tablespoon potato dough into a circle 2 inches in diameter. Place 1 level teaspoon of the curry filling in the center. Gather the sides and enclose filling. Roll into a ball between your palms, then roll the ball in breadcrumbs until it is well coated. With your fingers, shape it into a small pear. Insert a match-sized carrot stick into the small end to form a stem. Repeat with rest of dough and filling.*

COOKING: Heat 2 inches oil for deep-frying to 350 degrees. Fry dumplings in batches about 2 to 3 minutes until golden. Remove from oil and drain on paper towels. Cooked dumplings can be kept warm in a warm oven while the rest are being cooked.

NOTE: Uncooked dumplings can be kept in the refrigerator 1 day. Cooked dumplings can be kept in the refrigerator for several days, in the freezer for a few months. Reheat in 350-degree oven for 15 minutes or until heated through. Defrosting is not necessary; just heat a little longer than usual.

Taro Crescents

Makes 16 3-inch crescents, or 32 2½-inch crescents

Crispy outside and mousse-like inside, fried taro crescents are stuffed with tiny morsels of shrimp, pork and Chinese mushrooms. Small crescents make good hors d'oeuvres.

Taro is a starchy tuberous root of a tropical plant. Its texture is lighter than a potato's and has a special fragrance after cooking. The best kind to use for this recipe are the large taros with rough brown skin and white flesh interwoven with very fine purple fibers. Taro is available in Chinatown groceries year-round but is fairly perishable. The way to keep it is to steam it, as in this recipe, and freeze the steamed slices in a well-sealed plastic bag until ready to use. Blot dry after defrosting.

FILLING:

3 medium-size dry Chinese
　mushrooms
¼ cup bamboo shoots (or water
　chestnuts)

PORK MIXTURE:
¼ pound boneless pork in 1-inch
　cubes, or ground pork without
　processor
1 teaspoon cornstarch
1½ teaspoons soy sauce
1½ teaspoons dry sherry

SHRIMP MIXTURE:
¼ pound shrimp with shell
½ teaspoon cornstarch
⅛ teaspoon salt
1 teaspoon dry sherry

SAUCE MIXTURE:
¼ teaspoon salt or to taste
½ teaspoon sugar
⅛ teaspoon ground black pepper or
　to taste
1½ teaspoons dry sherry
1 tablespoon soy sauce
1½ teaspoons juice from mushrooms

1 tablespoon cooking oil
1½ teaspoons cornstarch in
　1 tablespoon water
1 teaspoon sesame oil

PREPARATION OF FILLING: Pour ½ cup boiling water over mushrooms and let soak about 20 minutes, until soft. Cut off and discard hard stems, then chop mushrooms into tiny pieces. Save juice for sauce mixture.

With steel blade in place, mince bamboo shoots with on/off turns. Do not overprocess. Remove from beaker.

With steel blade in place, process pork mixture with on/off turns until pork is minced. Remove from beaker.

Shell, devein and wash the shrimp. Then drain and pat dry with paper towels. Place shrimp mixture in beaker, and with steel blade process with a few quick on/off turns until shrimp is chopped. Do not overprocess.*

(Without food processor, mince bamboo and chop shrimp by hand. Mix pork mixture and shrimp mixture in separate bowls. Mix well.*)

COOKING OF FILLING: Heat wok over high heat, then heat 1 tablespoon oil until very hot. Cook pork until it almost loses its pink color; add chopped shrimp mixture, minced bamboo shoots and mushrooms. When shrimp is almost cooked, add sauce mixture. Stir to mix, then add cornstarch mixture and stir until thickened. Taste for seasoning; add more salt if desired. Add sesame oil, and mix well.*

NOTE: Filling can be made several days ahead and kept in refrigerator. Leftovers can be frozen.

TARO DOUGH:

1 pound taro, peeled and cut into ¼-inch slices
¼ cup cornstarch
6 tablespoons vegetable shortening or lard
1 teaspoon salt or to taste
2 teaspoons sugar
Boiling water, only if needed
Cooking oil for deep-frying

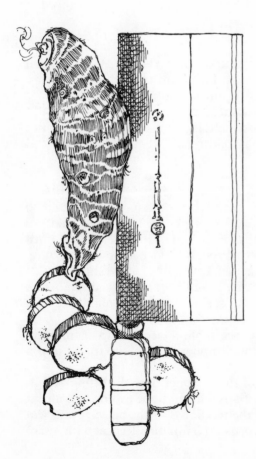

PREPARATION: Steam taro slices for 25 minutes or until soft.*

Place slices on cutting board and mash with a rolling pin. Discard hard pieces.

Mix taro with cornstarch, shortening, salt and sugar to form dough, and knead until the dough is smooth. If the dough is too dry, add just enough boiling water to form a workable dough.*

(You may use the food processor to mash the taro and blend with other ingredients, but when you fry the crescent, you will not get the interesting honeycomb-like texture on the surface.)

SHAPING: Divide the dough in half. For larger crescents, cut each portion into 8 pieces, and flatten pieces to circles 3 inches in diameter. For smaller crescents, cut each portion into 16 pieces, and flatten pieces to circles 2½ inches in diameter. Flatten with a lightly floured rolling pin on a lightly floured surface.

Place filling in the center of each circle, using 1 tablespoon for 3-inch crescents or 1½ teaspoons for 2-inch crescents.

Fold circles in half. Pinch and seal the edges tightly, making into 3-inch or 2½-inch crescents.*

COOKING: Heat 2 inches oil for deep-frying to 325 degrees. If oil temperature is too low, the dough will fall apart. If too hot, the dough will brown too quickly.

Fry the crescents in batches about 2 minutes until golden and crisp. Gently remove them from the oil. Drain on paper towels.*

NOTE: Uncooked crescents can be made 1 day ahead and kept in the refrigerator. Cooked crescents can be kept in the refrigerator for 4 to 5 days, in the freezer for several months. Reheat in preheated 300-degree oven for 20 minutes.

VARIATION: Potato may be used as a substitute for taro, but you will not get the sweetish fragrance characteristic of taro.

Spring Rolls (KNOWN AS EGG ROLLS BY AMERICANS)

Makes 16 rolls

This is the authentic version of egg rolls. Spring rolls are more delicate, lighter and crisper than egg rolls, and taste infinitely better. The secret lies in using the correct wrapper and better ingredients for the filling.

People in Shanghai always serve these on the Chinese New Year, for the shape of spring rolls resembles the gold bars used in the past as money; thus spring rolls symbolize wealth and prosperity.

Old or young, most Chinese like them, so they are served year round, usually as a snack. Cut in half, spring rolls make excellent hors d'oeuvres, or, served with a soup, a very satisfying meal.

The authentic Shanghai spring roll wrappers are traditionally round in shape and handmade by specialists. The Chinese do not normally make them at home. Nowadays, there are paper-thin square machine-made spring roll wrappers. They do not dry out as quickly as the handmade ones, and many find them easier to use. But do not mistake them for the square Cantonese egg roll wrappers, which are much heavier. Unfortunately, American supermarkets carry only the Cantonese egg roll wrappers; you'll have to get the Shanghai spring roll wrappers from Oriental food stores. The wrappers freeze very well, so you can stock up ahead of time, and just defrost before using.

SPRING ROLL FILLING:
½ **pound boneless, skinless chicken breast, shredded**

MARINADE:
2 teaspoons cornstarch
2 teaspoons dry sherry
2 teaspoons soy sauce

6 ounces frozen king crab meat, defrosted (or substitute ¼ pound shredded boiled ham)
5 tablespoons cooking oil
½ **pound celery cabbage (also known as Nappa cabbage), shredded**
1½ teaspoons salt or to taste
2 slices fresh ginger
½ **pound boiled ham, shredded**
6 ounces bamboo shoots, shredded (1½ cups)—winter bamboo shoots are best
3 scallions, finely shredded in 1½-inch lengths
1 tablespoon soy sauce

PREPARATION AND COOKING OF FILLING: Mix shredded chicken with marinade. If king crab is used, drain it very well. Cut large crabmeat chunks into smaller pieces.

Heat the wok, then heat 1 tablespoon oil until hot. Add cabbage and ¼ teaspoon salt, then stir-fry for 1 to 2 minutes until slightly soft. Do not overcook. Remove from wok and drain in colander.

Heat the wok, then heat 4 tablespoons oil until hot. Fry ginger slices for 1 minute. Discard ginger. Add chicken, stirring until chicken just turns white. Add ham, crab, bamboo shoots and scallions and return cooked cabbage. Add soy sauce, sugar and 1¼ teaspoons salt or to taste. Stir-fry until ingredients are heated through. Add cornstarch mixture, stirring until it is thickened. Let cool before wrapping.*

SHAPING: If there is any liquid in the filling, drain before wrapping, so filling won't soak the wrappers and make rolls soggy.

Lay the wrapper on the table. Place ¼ cup of filling in the lower center of the wrapper. Shape the filling into a cylinder.

Lift the lower flap of the wrapper over the filling, roll it, then fold in the 2 side flaps and continue rolling into a neat oblong package. Fold the top flap over the package and seal with a little water or cornstarch mixture. Repeat with rest of wrappers.

1 teaspoon sugar
1½ tablespoons cornstarch mixed
  with 3 tablespoon water
16 ready-made spring roll wrappers
2 cups cooking oil

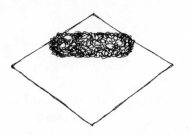

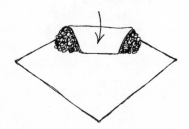

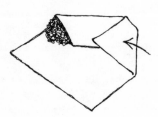 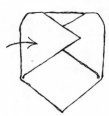 

Place the rolls sealed-side down. If they are not to be used right away, cover them with plastic wrap. If you stack them in layers, separate with wax paper in between.*

COOKING: Heat 2 cups of oil in a 10-inch skillet to 375 degrees.

Fry spring rolls in batches about 3 to 5 minutes, until golden and crisp on both sides. Remove and drain on paper towels. Cooked ones can be kept warm in a warm oven while the remainder are being fried.*

Serve hot with Chinese red vinegar, soy sauce or both. They are delicious with just Chinese red vinegar.

NOTE: Filling can be made 1 or 2 days ahead and kept in the refrigerator. Uncooked spring rolls can be made ½ day ahead and kept in the refrigerator or frozen for a few weeks. Do not defrost; fry directly in hot oil until golden outside and hot inside. Cooked ones can be kept in the refrigerator for a few days, in the freezer for a few weeks. Remove from plastic wrappers; defrost without overlapping each other, then fry in oil to recrisp.

VARIATION: You may use ready-made egg roll wrappers, although they are not as good, or to make your own egg roll wrappers see page 69.

Steamed Foods

Steaming is a very common method of cooking in Chinese kitchens, and one that has several advantages. It is clean cooking, for little or no oil is used so there is no splattering. And it is healthful cooking since the food's vitamins and minerals are preserved by the hot steam rather than boiled away. Many steamed foods can be cooked ahead and kept warm in the steamer over a low flame.

The traditional bamboo steamers come in several round layers that fit snugly over one another, and are made to be set onto a wok. The perforated woven bottoms allow steam to rise through the layers so that several dishes can be steamed at one time on the same burner. Steamers are quite attractive, so food can be served directly from them. Steamers of 12-inch to 13-inch diameter are best for 14-inch woks. They will also fit onto modern electric woks.

Western steamers can of course be substituted, or you can easily improvise from pots you have on hand. (See Steamer under *Equipment and Utensils*.)

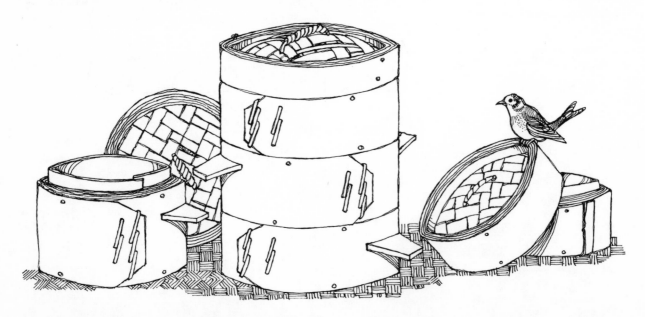

Steamed Beef Balls

These are called beef shao mai *in the teahouses. Chinese parsley and dried orange peel add interesting flavor to the beef in this recipe. However, the beef balls are delicious even without these special seasonings.*
Use toothpicks and serve them as hors d'oeuvres, or serve with a vegetable dish and rice as a main meal.

1 teaspoon dried orange peels (peels
   are available at Chinese groceries)
   or ½ teaspoon finely grated
   orange rind
2 large scallions, in 1-inch sections
1 tablespoon Chinese parsley (same
   as coriander or cilantro)
6 large water chestnuts
1 pound boneless beef, in 1-inch
   cubes, or ground lean beef
   without processor

SEASONING MIXTURE:
1 teaspoon salt or to taste
1 teaspoon sugar
2 teaspoons cornstarch
½ teaspoon ground black pepper
4 teaspoons soy sauce
2 tablespoons sesame oil

Lettuce leaves for lining the plates
   (optional)

PREPARATION: Soften dried orange peels in hot water, then mince by hand. With steel blade in place, mince scallions and Chinese parsley. Then add water chestnuts and coarsely chop with 2 quick on/off turns. Add beef cubes and chop with 3 quick on/off turns. Add seasoning mixture and minced orange peels, then process entire mixture with on/off turns until it is minced.

(Without food processor, mince scallions, parsley and water chestnuts by hand, then mix together with ground beef, seasoning mixture and minced orange peels in large bowl.)

With wet hands, shape beef mixture into 24 1-inch balls. Line heat-proof platter with lettuce leaves (optional) and place beef balls on top.*

COOKING: Bring water in the steamer to a rolling boil. Steam the beef balls for 8 to 10 minutes until just cooked.*

NOTE: Uncooked beef balls can be kept in the refrigerator for 1 day, in the freezer for several weeks. Cooked ones can also be refrigerated and frozen, but some flavor will be lost. They can be resteamed or reheated in a microwave oven.

Crab Meat and Shrimp Dumplings

Makes 32

These open-topped dumplings, known as shao mai *in Cantonese, are very popular in teahouses. The crab meat and shrimp in this recipe add delicious flavor and give a lighter texture than the more commonly served pork filling. These dumplings are easy to make and are wonderful as hors d'oeuvres, or even as a meal, when accompanied by a soup.*

Wonton wrappers are now available in many American supermarkets, and they can be bought ahead and kept in the freezer. They come in different thicknesses. The thin ones make more delicate dumplings and are better for this recipe. Though restaurants use round wrappers, if they are not available the thin square wonton wrappers are just as good, and it is not necessary to trim them down to circles before wrapping.

2 cubes fresh ginger, ½ inch each
2 scallions, white tops only
¼ pound boneless pork in 1-inch cubes, or ground pork without processor
4 large water chestnuts, cut into halves
½ pound shrimp with shell

SEASONING MIXTURE:
1 teaspoon sugar
1¼ teaspoons salt or to taste
1 tablespoon soy sauce
2 tablespoons sesame oil
1 tablespoon dry sherry
1 egg white
4 teaspoons cornstarch

PREPARATION: With steel blade in place, mince ginger and scallions. Then add pork and water chestnuts and process until minced. Remove ingredients from beaker.

Shell, devein and wash the shrimp. Then drain and pat dry with paper towels.

With steel blade in place, coarsely chop shrimp with on/off turns.

(Without food processor, mince and chop ingredients by hand.)

In a bowl, add seasoning mixture and all the minced and chopped ingredients. Mix thoroughly by hand, then add crab. Toss gently until just mixed.*

SHAPING: Place 1 level tablespoon of filling in the center of a wrapper. Gather the sides of the wrapper around the filling to pleat naturally. Make sure the wrapper sticks to the filling, and the dumpling stands upright. Repeat the process with remaining filling and wrappers.*

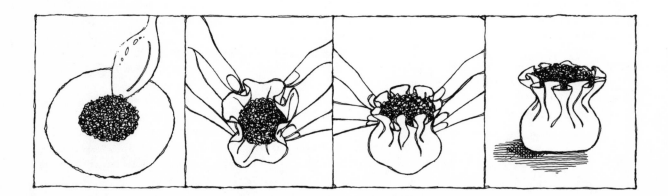

¼ pound crab meat (fresh or pasteurized blue crab meat, or use king crab meat, defrosted, drained and coarsely chopped)

32 thin ready-made wonton wrappers, 3-inch round or 3-inch square (or to make the wrappers yourself, see page 69)

Oil a heatproof plate at least 1 inch smaller in diameter than the steamer. If a bamboo steamer is used, either oil the rack or line the rack with lettuce leaves. Place dumplings on the top.*

STEAMING: Bring water in the steamer to a rolling boil. Steam the dumpling for 20 minutes. Serve directly from the bamboo steamer or the plate, and serve with soy sauce and Chinese red rice vinegar if desired.*

NOTE: Dumplings can be made 1 day ahead and kept in the refrigerator before cooking, or in the freezer for several weeks. Cooked ones can be rewarmed by steaming, but some flavor will be lost.

Glutinous Rice Dumplings

Makes 32

Glutinous rice is shorter grained than ordinary rice. It also has a sweeter taste than ordinary rice and, after cooking, the grains stick to each other; therefore, it is called "sweet" or "sticky" rice. It is not eaten as ordinary rice; rather, it is used in sweet foods or as stuffing, as in this recipe.

FILLING:
1 cup glutinous rice
2 tablespoons dry shrimp
3 dry Chinese mushrooms
¼ pound Chinese pork sausages (about 4 links, or use cooked ham for substitute)
4 small water chestnuts
½ teaspoon sugar
3 tablespoons soy sauce or to taste
1 tablespoon dry sherry

32 thin ready-made wonton wrappers, 3-inch round or 3-inch square (or to make your own wrappers, see page 69)

PREPARATION OF FILLING: Wash the rice in cold water and drain in a strainer. Repeat 2 or 3 times. Drain the rice very well, and place it in a 2-quart saucepan. Add 1 cup water. Bring to a boil on high heat, then cook for about 2 minutes or until most of the water is absorbed. Reduce to very low heat, cover the saucepan and cook for 10 minutes. Remove from heat, and let stand covered for 10 minutes.

While the rice is cooking, pour boiling water over dry shrimp and mushrooms in separate bowls and let soak about 20 minutes or until soft. Cut off and discard hard stems from mushrooms, and chop mushrooms and shrimp. Chop Chinese sausages and water chestnuts. Add shrimp, mushrooms, sausages, water chestnuts and remaining filling ingredients to cooked rice and mix well.

SHAPING: (See illustration for Crab Meat and Shrimp Dumplings.) Place 1 heaping tablespoon of filling in the center of a wrapper. Gather the sides of the wrapper around the filling to pleat naturally. Make sure the wrapper sticks to the filling, and the dumpling stands upright. Repeat the process with remaining filling and wrappers.*

Oil 2 heatproof plates at least 1 inch smaller in diameter than the steamer. If a bamboo steamer is used, either oil the rack or line the rack with lettuce leaves. Place dumplings on top.

COOKING: Bring water in the steamer to a rolling boil. Steam the dumplings for 20 minutes. Serve directly from the bamboo steamer or the plates. Serve hot with soy sauce if desired.*

NOTE: Dumplings can be made 1 day ahead and kept in the refrigerator. Cover tightly with plastic wrap to prevent wrapper from drying. Cooked ones can be kept in the refrigerator for 2 to 3 days, in the freezer for several weeks. Make sure they are tightly sealed. Rewarm by steaming; defrosting is not necessary.

Steamed Yeast Dough

Makes 16 stuffed buns

The yeast dough used in steamed buns is quite similar to Western yeast bread dough. However, unlike baked buns, which are brownish, steamed buns are whitish in appearance.

Stuffed steamed buns are one of the most popular snacks in China. The stuffing can be either sweet or salty. Sweet stuffings can be made from red bean paste, date paste, lotus seed paste, or black sesame seeds. Salty stuffings are often chicken, pork or pork with vegetables.

Many Chinese families make steamed buns at home. Steamed buns sold in stores are made in different shapes or decorated with red stamps to distinguish the different stuffings.

1 cup warm water (about
  110 degrees)
1 teaspoon dry yeast
1 tablespoon sugar
3 cups all-purpose flour
2 tablespoons vegetable shortening
1 teaspoon baking powder

PREPARATION: Place ¼ cup of warm water in a small bowl, then sprinkle yeast over the water. Sprinkle sugar over yeast. Let stand for 10 minutes, or until yeast has reacted and doubled in bulk.

With steel blade or short plastic dough blade in place, add flour, then vegetable shortening to the beaker. Process until mixed. Add yeast mixture, and process again until mixed. With the machine running, add ¾ cup warm water through feed tube. Process until a ball of dough forms on the blades. If the ball is not forming, add a little more water. Or, if the dough is too wet, add a little more flour. If a plastic dough blade is used, knead ball of dough in processor for 1 minute. Otherwise, knead dough by hand on lightly floured surface for 2 to 3 minutes.

(Without food processor, mix flour, vegetable shortening, yeast mixture and water together by hand, then knead for about 10 minutes or until dough is smooth.)

Place dough in a bowl at least twice its size, and cover with plastic wrap. Leave in a warm place from 1 to 2 hours, depending on the surrounding temperature, until dough has doubled in bulk.

Remove dough from the bowl. Knead with baking powder by hand for 2 to 3 minutes, until the baking powder is mixed in. Dough is now ready for shaping.

Steamed Roast Pork Buns

Makes 16

Char shiu bao *is the Cantonese name for these buns, which are specialties of the teahouses. Eat them as snacks, or serve them at a buffet. They even make a nice light meal when served with soup. Chinese people often buy these buns ready-made at specialty stores, then resteam them at home.*

**1 recipe Steamed Yeast Dough
  (page 43)
1 recipe Roast Pork Filling
  (page 52)
16 2-inch-square pieces wax paper**

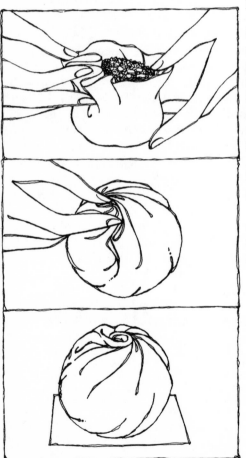

PREPARATION AND SHAPING: Prepare yeast dough and pork filling as directed.

Divide yeast dough in half. On a lightly floured surface, roll each half into a cylinder about 1½ inches in diameter. Cut each cylinder into 8 equal portions. To prevent dough from drying out, keep portions in a bowl and covered with plastic wrap until ready to shape.

On a lightly floured surface, roll 1 portion into a circle 3½ inches in diameter, with the edges of the circle slightly thinner than the center. Divide the filling into 16 portions or place 1 generous tablespoon of pork filling in the center of the circle. Pull and gather the edges of dough to enclose the filling, pleating as you go along. Bring pleated edges together and twist to seal. Place bun pleated side up on a 2-inch square of wax paper. Prepare other buns in the same manner. Cover with dry cloth and let rise for 20 minutes.

COOKING: Bring water for steaming to a rolling boil. Place buns on bamboo steamers or steamer rack about 2 inches apart. Steam over high heat for 20 minutes. Serve hot.*

NOTE: Cooked buns can be kept in the refrigerator for several days, in the freezer for 1 to 2 months. Thawing is not necessary; just resteam for 15 minutes or until piping hot inside.

Steamed Red Bean Paste Buns

Red bean paste is the most popular sweet filling for steamed buns.

**1 recipe Steamed Yeast Dough
  (page 43)**
1½ cups red bean paste, canned
16 2-inch-square pieces wax paper

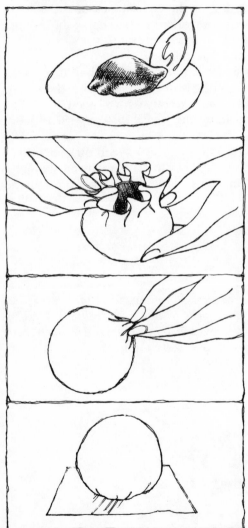

PREPARATION AND SHAPING: Prepare yeast dough as direct-ed. Divide dough in half. On a lightly floured surface, roll each half into a cylinder about 1½ inches in diameter. Cut each cylinder into 8 equal portions. To prevent dough from drying out, keep portions in a bowl and covered with plastic wrap until ready to shape.

On a lightly floured surface, roll 1 portion into a circle 3½ inches in diameter with a rolling pin, keeping edges of the circle slightly thinner than the center. Place 1 heaping table-spoon of red bean paste in the center of the circle. Pull and gather the edges of dough to enclose the filling. Place the bun sealed side down on a 2-inch square of wax paper. Prepare other buns in the same manner. Cover with dry cloth and let rise for 20 minutes.

COOKING: Bring water for steaming to a rolling boil. Place buns on bamboo steamers or steamer rack about 2 inches apart. Steam over high heat for 20 minutes. Serve warm.*

NOTE: Cooked buns can be kept in the refrigerator for over a week, in the freezer for 2 to 3 months. Thawing is not neces-sary; just resteam for 15 minutes or until hot inside.

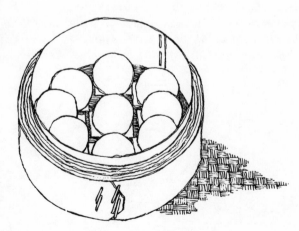

Wheat Starch Dough

Makes 48 dumplings

When the gluten part of wheat flour is removed, the remaining part is called wheat starch. The resulting dough is used to make the wrappers for delicate dumplings, and it will crack if not handled with care since the dough is not elastic. It also becomes translucent after steaming, and if the dough is made very thin, the color of the stuffing will show through the wrapper. Wheat starch is available in any Chinese grocery store and from mail-order sources.

2 cups wheat starch
1 teaspoon salt
1½ cups water
2 tablespoons cooking oil

PREPARATION: (Because of the consistency of the dough, the food processor does not work as well as doing the mixing and kneading by hand.)

Mix wheat starch and salt in bowl.

Measure 1½ cups water, and bring it to a boil in a small pot. Quickly pour the boiling water all at once into the wheat starch mixture. Stir and mix quickly with a spoon.

Add the oil, and knead by hand until the dough is soft and smooth.

Divide the dough into quarters. Roll each quarter into a cylinder 1 inch in diameter. They are now ready for shaping, or place in the bowl and cover with plastic wrap until ready to use.

Steamed Shrimp Dumplings (*Har Gow*)

Makes 48

Har gow is the Cantonese name for shrimp dumplings. These delicate dumplings with pinkish-colored shrimp showing through a white translucent dough are one of the favorite teahouse specialties of the Chinese. The shrimp used should be as fresh as possible. Shrimp dumplings are lightly seasoned so the natural fresh flavor of the shrimp can be tasted. Care should be taken not to overcook the dumplings.

SHRIMP FILLING:
¾ pound shrimp with shells
2 cubes fresh ginger, ½ inch each
   (about 2 teaspoons finely minced)
1 scallion, white top only, cut into
   2 sections crosswise
7 water chestnuts
2 teaspoons cornstarch
1½ teaspoons salt or to taste
1 teaspoon sugar
2 teaspoons dry sherry
1 tablespoon sesame oil

1 recipe Wheat Starch Dough (see
   page 46)

SOY AND SESAME OIL DIP:
2 tablespoons soy sauce
2 teaspoons sesame oil

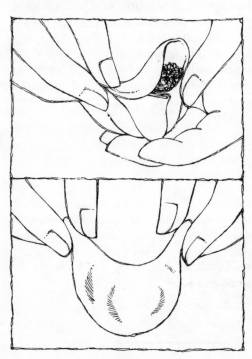

PREPARATION: Shell, devein and wash the shrimp. Then drain and pat dry with paper towels.

With steel blade in place, mince ginger and scallion top very finely. Add water chestnuts, and chop coarsely with on/off turns. Then add shrimp and remaining ingredients for the filling. With a few quick on/off turns, process only until shrimp is coarsely chopped. Do not overprocess.*

(Without food processor, mince ginger and scallion very finely by hand, and mince water chestnuts to the size of rice. Dice shrimp to the size of peas. Mix all the filling ingredients together.*)

SHAPING: Lightly oil a Chinese cleaver or a pastry scraper, then cut 1 of the 4 cylinders of wheat starch dough into 12 equal portions. Again lightly oil 1 side of the cleaver or pastry scraper, and oil a small edge of a working table or a wood cutting board. Flatten 1 of the 12 portions of dough between the oiled surfaces of the cleaver and the table, pressing the cleaver evenly with your palm until the dough is a circle or oval about 2½ inches in diameter.

Pick the dough up carefully, with the blade of a small knife, if necessary. With your thumb and forefinger, form pleats along 1 side of the dough. After 5 or 6 pleats, the wrapper will shape into a pouch. Fill the pouch with 1 teaspoon of shrimp filling. Press the pleated and unpleated sides of the dough firmly together. Seal the edges tightly. Dumpling should be in a crescent shape. Repeat with rest of dough and filling.*

COOKING: Place dumplings on an oiled platter, then place platter in a preboiled steamer. Cover and steam for 8 minutes or until shrimp is just cooked. Do not oversteam. Serve hot with Chinese red vinegar or with soy and sesame oil dip.

NOTE: Uncooked dumplings can be kept in the refrigerator for ½ day. Cover with plastic wrap. If fresh shrimp is used, uncooked dumplings can be frozen for 1 to 2 months. Cooked dumplings can be kept in the refrigerator for a few days or be frozen. You can rewarm by steaming, but much flavor is lost upon recooking.

Roasted and Baked Foods

Since the oven is not standard equipment in traditional Chinese kitchens, roasting and baking have usually been done by restaurants and specialty stores. Although many Chinese homes in Hong Kong now have modern cooking facilities, roasted and baked foods remain commercial specialties, and very few Chinese prepare them at home. The practice of eating roasted delicacies in the restaurants and buying ready-roasted and ready-baked foods from specialty stores is as prevalent in China today as it was centuries ago.

This tradition is also practiced among the Chinese abroad. Roast pork displayed in store windows is a typical scene in Chinatowns. Each store does the roasting daily on its own premises, and each has its well-guarded secret ingredients. The meat is usually roasted in a vertical position so it will be more evenly exposed to the heat in the oven; in this way, too, the fat drains off more effectively. Roast pork is sold by weight, and is so popular that it is usually sold out before the end of the day.

Chinese bakeries in Chinatowns also enjoy flourishing business. Windows and display cases of these bakeries are filled with colorful and intriguing geometric shapes, with pastries baked in figures like buddhas or fish. Some are from centuries-old recipes, others are modern creations inspired and influenced by Western bakeries. Chinese baked goods are either sweet concoctions or pastries with savory meat stuffings. Some of the popular ones are included in this chapter.

Chinese Roast Pork   *Serves 8-12*

When marinated with Chinese seasonings and spices, pork becomes one of the tastiest and finest choices of meat. Chinese roast pork is a very versatile food—delicious sliced or served cold as an appetizer, excellent in rice and noodle dishes, and equally good in stir-fried dishes or used as fillings for dim sum.

You may want to roast more pork than you need and freeze some for use in other recipes in this book.

For this recipe, pork should be marinated overnight.

3 pounds boneless pork butt

MARINADE:
¼ cup ketchup
¼ cup hoisin sauce
¼ cup dry sherry
¼ cup soy sauce
2 cloves garlic, peeled and crushed
2 slices fresh ginger, shredded
1 teaspoon salt or to taste
1½ tablespoons sugar

"S"-shaped hooks made from stiff wire, or curtain hooks or paper clips bent into "S" shape
¼ cup light corn syrup
1 large roasting pan for catching drippings

PREPARATION: Trim off excess fat from meat. Cut pork into ¾-inch-thick by 2-inch-wide by 4-inch to 5-inch-long strips.

Mix the marinade ingredients together in a large bowl. Marinate meat, making sure all the surfaces of each piece of pork are covered. Let stand overnight in the refrigerator, turning the meat around a few times.*

COOKING: Preheat oven to 375 degrees. Place 1 oven rack close to the top of the oven, another rack closest to the bottom. Fill a large roasting pan with ½-inch water and place it on the bottom rack.

Drain the marinade from the meat, then push a hook into each strip of meat. Pull out the top rack, so it will be easier for hanging, and hang the other end of the hooks onto the rack. (Space so pieces of meat do not touch each other.) The meat also should not touch the water in the pan, and should not hang over the edges of the pan, so the pan can catch all the drippings and prevent smoking.

Roast the pork at 375 degrees for 50 minutes or until the pork is cooked. Overcooking will make the pork dry and tough.

To get a nice glaze, brush the hot meat with light corn syrup after it is removed from the oven.*

Cut into thin slices. Serve warm or cold.

NOTE: Cooked roast pork can be kept in the refrigerator for 4 or 5 days, in the freezer for 1 to 2 months. It is better to leave the meat in whole pieces for storing or rewarming in the oven.

To get the red color like the roast pork sold in the Chinese grocery stores, add red food coloring to the marinade.

Flaky Pastry Dough

Flaky pastry dough is similar to Western puff pastry because it too consists of layers and layers of paper-thin dough. However, it does not puff up and is not crisp like puff pastry; it is tender and flaky, and more close to the texture of pie crust.

Making the pastry dough is a mechanical process. Once you have learned it, you'll find it easier to work with than the Western puff pastry, for no refrigeration or periods of waiting are necessary. But do not overwork, and roll the dough with a minimum of pressure.

This recipe can easily be doubled, and processed in one batch in a regular food processor.

INNER DOUGH:
¾ cup all-purpose flour
½ cup vegetable shortening or lard

OUTER DOUGH:
1 cup all-purpose flour
½ teaspoon salt (optional)
2 tablespoons vegetable shortening
  or lard
1 large egg
2 tablespoons water

PREPARATION: With steel blade in place, add flour and shortening for the inner dough mixture to the beaker. Process until the dough just clings together. On a lightly floured surface, shape dough into a roll and set aside.

With steel blade in place, add flour, salt and shortening for the outer dough mixture to the beaker. Process until mixed. Add egg and water, and process until a ball of dough is formed. Add more water if the dough is too dry. Process the dough for another minute; it should be soft and pliable. Cover the dough in a bowl with plastic wrap, and let stand for at least 15 minutes before using.*

(Without food processor, mix ingredients for inner dough with a fork until well mixed. Set aside. Mix ingredients for outer dough together, adding more water if the dough is too dry. On a lightly floured surface, knead outer dough for 8 to 10 minutes or until dough is smooth and elastic. Cover the dough in a bowl with plastic wrap and let stand for at least 15 minutes before using.)*

SHAPING: Divide each portion of dough into 16 equal portions. On a lightly floured surface, with a rolling pin, roll 1 portion of the outer dough into a 3 by 4-inch oval with the edges thinner than the center portion. Shape 1 portion of the inner dough into a roll 2½ inches long, and place at the center of the outer dough.

Wrap the outer dough so it will totally enclose the inner dough. Place seam-side down, and, on a lightly floured surface, roll out lengthwise into a 7-inch-long strip. Then, beginning at one end, roll the strip up into a cylinder. Roll the cylinder out lengthwise, and once again roll up into a cylinder.

With your hands make the dough into a round shape, then with a rolling pin roll into a circle 4 or 5 inches in diameter, or a 3½-inch square. Repeat with the other portions.*

NOTE: Both inner and outer dough, as well as the finished pastry dough, can be kept in the refrigerator for a few days, in the freezer for a few weeks. Make sure they are sealed tightly in plastic bags. Bring to room temperature before using.

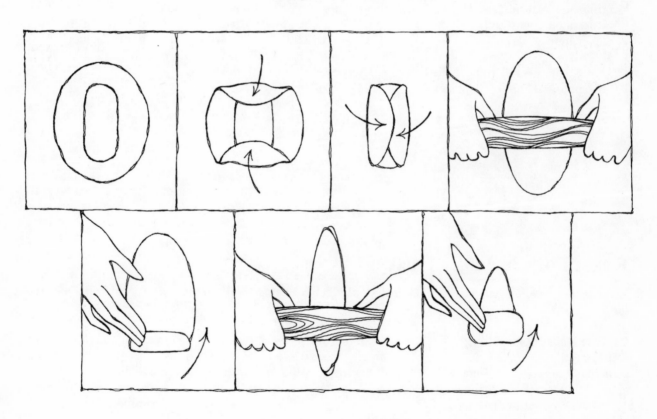

Roast Pork Filling

Makes 1½ cups (for 16 buns)

This savory filling is a classic. Subtly seasoned, with a sweetish taste, this time-honored Chinese roast pork is further enhanced by a richly flavored oyster sauce that makes a wonderful filling for buns and pastries. You can double the recipe and easily make it in larger quantities, for use in steamed and baked buns, or in flaky pastries.

½ pound Chinese Roast Pork (page 48, or purchase cooked pork in food stores in Chinatown)
2 tablespoons oyster-flavored sauce
1 tablespoon soy sauce or to taste
1½ tablespoons sugar or to taste
½ tablespoon all-purpose flour
½ tablespoon cornstarch
¼ cup water
1 tablespoon cooking oil
1 clove garlic, peeled and crushed
1 tablespoon sesame oil (optional)

PREPARATION: Cut Chinese roast pork into ⅛-inch slices, then cut the slices into ¼ by ½-inch pieces.

Mix oyster-flavored sauce, soy sauce, sugar, flour and cornstarch in a bowl until smooth and free of lumps. Then add water and mix thoroughly.*

COOKING: Heat 1 tablespoon oil in a wok over medium heat, sauté garlic for 30 seconds and discard. Give the sauce mixture a good stir to recombine it, then add to the wok. Heat and stir constantly until the sauce has thickened.

Add roast pork. Cook and mix thoroughly until the sauce is coated evenly over the pork and is very thick. Add sesame oil. Let cook before using.*

NOTE: Roast pork filling can be kept in the refrigerator for several days. Excess filling can be kept in the freezer for several weeks.

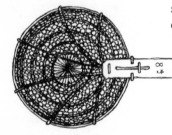

Roast Pork in Flaky Pastry

Makes 24

These tender and flaky pastries filled with roast pork make wonderful finger snacks. They are also good for buffets or picnics.

1 recipe Roast Pork Filling (page 52)
2 recipes Flaky Pastry Dough (page 50)—makes 32 (for a quick and easy variation, see Variation below)
1 egg yolk mixed with 1 teaspoon cream or milk

SHAPING: Process 2 recipes of flaky pastry dough together in 1 batch with food processor, or by hand. Divide both the inner and outer dough into 32 equal portions.

Shape the inner and outer dough as in flaky pastry dough recipe into either circles 4 inches in diameter or 3½-inch squares.

Place 1 level tablespoon roast pork filling in the center of the dough. Brush the edges with egg yolk mixture or with

water, then fold the circle or square in half. Press the edges together to seal tightly.

Brush the top of the pastry with egg yolk mixture. Prepare remaining pastries in the same manner.* (Filling is enough for 24 pastries; excess dough can be frozen for future use.)

BAKING: Preheat oven to 375 degrees and bake for 25 minutes or until golden. Can be served warm or cold.*

NOTE: Unbaked stuffed pastry can be kept in the refrigerator for 1 day, in the freezer for many weeks. Baked pastry can be kept in the refrigerator for several days, in the freezer for many weeks. Bake or rewarm in the oven. Defrosting is not necessary, just bake a little longer.

VARIATION: (Makes 24) For an easy and quick modern variation, use frozen ready-to-use puff pastry available in the supermarkets. It comes in a 17¼-ounce package in 2 pre-rolled sheets. This puff pastry will give a crisper and more puffy pastry, but it is also delicious.

Defrost puff pastry for 30 minutes or until it is softer and can be unfolded easily. Each of the 2 sheets measures 9 by 10 inches.

Cut each sheet along folds, making 3 rectangles about 3 by 10 inches, then cut each rectangle into 4 equal pieces about 2½ by 3 inches. You will have 12 pieces from each sheet, or a total of 24 from 2 sheets.

On a lightly floured surface, with a rolling pin roll each piece into a 3½-inch square. Place 1 level tablespoon of filling in the center of 1 square. Brush the edges with egg yolk mixture, and fold the square into a triangle. Press the edges together to seal. Brush the top with egg yolk mixture. Repeat the process with the rest of the pastry and filling.

Bake in a preheated 375-degree oven for 30 minutes or until crust is baked and golden.*

They can be made ahead and rewarmed as with flaky pastry.

Curry Puffs

These puffs are wonderful finger food, and can be served either warm or at room temperature. Accompanied by a soup, they make a nice light meal. Like Roast Pork in Flaky Pastry, they can be made far in advance and therefore are a good party food. For a quick and easy variation, use frozen ready-to-use puff pastry available in the freezer section of the supermarket; it is crisper and puffier than flaky pastry. One 17¼-ounce package will make 24 puffs.

You may use beef or pork for the curry filling.

**2 recipes Flaky Pastry Dough
(page 50; for a quick variation,
see Variation under Roast Pork in
Flaky Pastry)**
2 recipes Curry Filling (page 32)

**2 egg yolks mixed with 2 teaspoons
cream or milk**

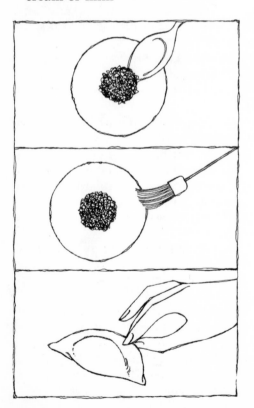

PREPARATION AND SHAPING: Process 2 recipes of flaky pastry dough together in one batch, with food processor or by hand. Divide both the inner and outer dough into 32 equal portions. Shape the dough as in flaky pastry dough recipe into either circles 4 inches in diameter or 3½-inch squares.

Cook 2 recipes of curry filling in one batch also.

Place 1 level tablespoon of curry filling in the center of dough. Brush the edges with egg yolk mixture or water, then fold the circle or square in half. Press the edges together to seal tightly. Brush the top of the pastry with egg yolk mixture. Repeat with rest of dough and filling.*

BAKING: Preheat oven to 375 degrees and bake for 25 minutes or until golden. Serve either warm or at room temperature.*

NOTE: Unbaked filled pastry can be kept in the refrigerator for 1 day, in the freezer for several weeks. Baked pastry can be kept in the refrigerator for several days, in the freezer for many weeks. Bake or rewarm in the oven. Defrosting is not necessary; just bake a little longer than usual.

Coconut Tarts

These tarts of golden toasted coconut in a light egg custard are consumed mostly as between-meal snacks by the Chinese, but are equally good served as dessert Western style. They can be eaten cold, but warm ones taste better—just reheat in the oven before serving.

FILLING:

1⅛ cups sugar, or to taste

¾ cup water

4 eggs

4 teaspoons cornstarch mixed with ¼ cup water

1½ cups unsweetened coconut shreds (available in health food stores)

1 recipe Flaky Pastry Dough (page 50, or for quick substitute see Variation below)

12 3½-inch-wide by 1½-inch-deep brioche molds or large muffin tins

PREPARATION: Heat sugar and water in saucepan until sugar is dissolved. Cool to room temperature.

Lightly beat the eggs with steel blade of food processor, using quick on/off turns or with an electric mixer at low speed. Then add sugar solution and cornstarch mixture, and process or beat until the ingredients are mixed. Do not overmix—it will create a lot of air bubbles. Stir in coconut shreds.*

SHAPING: Prepare flaky pastry dough as in recipe, and shape pastry into circles 4½ to 5 inches in diameter. If your muffin tins are smaller than the size specified above, shape smaller circles and use less filling.

Fit each circle into a mold, pressing it along the sides and bottom. Trim off any excess pastry along the edge.

Give the filling mixture a good stir to recombine ingredients. Measure ¼ cup and pour into 1 mold. Repeat with rest of filling.*

BAKING: Preheat oven to 375 degrees and bake for 30 to 40 minutes until coconut is golden brown. Remove tarts from mold before serving. If desired, place them in paper baking cups.*

NOTE: Tarts can be kept in the refrigerator for several days, or can be frozen. Reheat in 325-degree oven before serving.

VARIATION: For quick pastry dough, use frozen ready-to-use puff pastry available in supermarkets. There are 2 9-by-10-inch sheets in a 17¼-ounce package. Defrost 1 sheet, and cut into 12 pieces, each measuring 2½ by 3 inches. On lightly floured surface, with a rolling pin roll each piece into a 4½-inch square, then cut to a circle 4½ inches in diameter. Fit the circles into molds, pressing them along the sides and bottom. Trim off any excess pastry along the edges. Prick the bottom and sides of puff pastries very well with tines of fork to prevent them from puffing during baking. (Here we do not want the pastry to puff up.) Give the filling mixture a good stir. Pour ¼ cup into each pastry.

QUICK ONE-DISH MEALS

快餐

In addition to dim sum, Chinese teahouses offer noodle and rice dishes topped or mixed with a variety of meat and vegetables. These dishes are served at lunchtime, as well as in the evening when most teahouses turn into regular Cantonese restaurants. They are also perfect to cook at home, for you can keep your budget in check with these self-contained meals. Expensive meat and seafood go further when cooked with rice, noodles and vegetables. One-dish meals can be fried rice with assorted ingredients, another wonderful way to use up leftovers—or just simply take a portion of boiled rice and top it with a savory dish.

Noodles can be crispy pan-fried, soft-fried or in soup, and are prepared with meat and vegetables. Chinese noodles come in great varieties—soft freshly made and dry wheat flour noodles, fresh and dry egg noodles, thin dry rice flour noodles (rice sticks), soft and slippery fresh rice flour noodles. Their shapes range from fine threads to ribbon-sized.

With this choice of noodles, and the combinations of sauces and toppings, there are countless one-dish meals you can create. Western pasta dishes have been extremely popular these days, but Americans are just beginning to discover the dimensions of Chinese noodle dishes.

Stir-Fried Foods

Many of the dishes in this chapter are cooked by stir-frying, a unique Chinese cooking method that is particularly relevant to today's cooking needs. All the preparations of the ingredients can be done ahead, and because stir-fry cooking takes little time, it is perfect for quick meals and has the added benefit of producing crisp vegetables and tender juicy meat without losing flavor and nutrients.

Since stir-fried cooking is so fast, it is important that the ingredients be cut to small and uniform bite-sizes so they will cook evenly. It is also a good practice to read through all the cooking steps before heating the oil and have all the ingredients ready, because there will be no time to hunt for them once cooking begins. Arrange the ingredients near the stove in the order in which they are to be added to the wok, or arrange them clockwise on a tray.

Although the wok is the most convenient utensil for stir-frying, you can also use a heavy skillet. It is important that the wok be very hot before the oil is added, and the oil be hot before the food is added. The food should sizzle when placed in the oil, then should be stirred constantly and tossed with a spatula so that all parts of it come in contact with the hottest part of the pan. The rounded bottom of the wok makes it easier for these motions. Usually meat and vegetables are cooked separately before combining, since they have different cooking times. To prevent overcooking, remove the food from the heat quickly after the cooking is completed. Stir-fried dishes taste best when served immediately.

To ensure tender and flavorful meat, chicken or seafood, watch for its color, and cook until it just loses all of the raw meat color. You want the meat just cooked but not overcooked. Vegetables should not be overcooked either, but should retain their crisp texture. The cooking times in the recipes are only approximations, and will vary since your heat may be stronger or weaker.

Do not overload the wok; it is better to limit the amounts of meat, chicken or seafood to one pound for each batch, since regular stoves are usually not strong enough to supply the necessary heat for larger quantities, and you will end up with a stew. Stir-frying is so fast that, if you want to double the recipe, just cook it in two batches. On the other hand, half a recipe cooks very well.

In the beginning, you should follow the recipe carefully, so you will know how a properly cooked dish should look and taste. But once you have mastered the dish, start improvising with ingredients you have on hand. Flexibility is the advantage of Chinese cooking. You'll find it handy to have fresh ginger, scallion and fresh vegetables in the refrigerator and some meat and chicken in the freezer (for freezing information, see page 16). It is also a good idea to have soy sauce, dry sherry, cornstarch and canned chicken broth in the kitchen, for you can create many impromptu meals once you are familiar with the techniques of stir-frying. And there are almost limitless combinations of meat, poultry, seafood and vegetables for you to try.

Boiled Rice

There are two kinds of rice available in American supermarkets: long grain rice and medium grain rice. Both can be used for boiled rice; it is just a matter of personal preference. Long grain rice has a lighter and more fluffy texture, and is better for making fried rice. Medium grain rice has a softer and more sticky texture.

Always cook rice in a pot that has a tight-fitting cover and is at least four times larger than the amount of rice to be cooked.

The Chinese usually wash rice several times to rinse off any loose starch before cooking. Most rice in America is now enriched and specially labeled "to retain vitamins, do not rinse before cooking." (This enriched rice has less superficial starch; you can get good results without washing it, and save time too.)

If you do wash the rice, drain it very well, then add the appropriate amount of water. Place rice and water in the pot, then heat uncovered over high heat until it comes to a vigorous boil. Turn the heat down immediately to very low and cover the pot. (On an electric stove, transfer the pot to another burner that is preheated at low, instead of leaving it on the same burner and waiting for burner to cool.) Let it simmer for 20 to 25 minutes undisturbed. Then immediately remove the pot from the heat, and let it stand for at least 10 minutes. It is important not to open the pot throughout the simmering and standing periods. The heat in the pot will finish cooking the rice during the standing period. Fluff rice up before serving.

The following are ratios of rice to water. Add a little more water for softer rice, use less for firmer rice. One cup uncooked rice makes about 3½ cups cooked rice.

LONG GRAIN RICE	WATER
1 cup	1½ cups
2 cups	3 cups
3 cups	4 cups
MEDIUM GRAIN RICE	WATER
1 cup	1⅓ cups
2 cups	2½ cups
3 cups	3½ cups

NOTE: Freshly cooked rice will stay warm in the pot for a good half hour, or keep warm in a warm oven. Cooked rice can be kept in the refrigerator for 5 or 6 days, in the freezer for a long time. You can save time and fuel by cooking extra amounts of rice, and refrigerating or freezing for future use. Rice can be rewarmed by steaming directly in a heatproof serving bowl, or reheated quickly in a microwave oven. (See page 21.)

If you eat rice frequently, you might want to buy an automatic rice cooker. This comes in many different sizes. It will cook the rice, then keep it warm in the cooker.

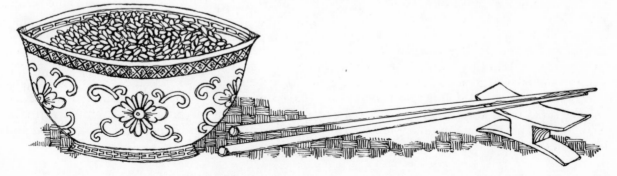

Subgum Fried Rice

Serves 3 to 4 as one-dish meal

The Chinese often eat fried rice as an afternoon snack, for it is a good way of using leftover rice and meat. In Cantonese, subgum means "an assortment of ingredients." The ingredients can be as varied as you like; if, for instance, you don't have fresh bean sprouts, you may substitute shredded lettuce or defrosted frozen green peas or skip the vegetable altogether. Chinese sausages and Chinese roast pork, though not necessary, not only add color to the dish, but also enhance the flavor of the rice. Use either one or both. If you are able to get them, stock up in your refrigerator or freezer. Or when you are making your own Chinese roast pork (see page 48), make an extra amount for your future fried rice dishes. A good fried rice should be light and aromatic. Always use cold cooked rice with grains individually separated.

5 large fresh mushrooms, diced (or dry Chinese mushrooms)
¾ cup cooked meat, diced (chicken, shrimp, crab meat, Chinese sausages or roast pork)
¾ cup ham, diced
3 large eggs
1 teaspoon salt or to taste
4½ tablespoons cooking oil
2 scallions, chopped
2 cups fresh bean sprouts, washed and drained
4 cups cold cooked rice
1 tablespoon soy sauce or to taste

PREPARATION: If dry Chinese mushrooms are used, pour ½ cup boiling water over them and let soak about 20 minutes or until soft. Cut off and discard hard stems, then cut mushrooms into dice.

If Chinese sausages are used, steam 2 links for 15 minutes. Then slice or chop before cooking with rice.

Beat eggs with ¼ teaspoon salt or to taste.

HAVE READY BEFORE COOKING:
1. Cooking oil
2. Beaten eggs
3. Scallion, bean sprouts, mushrooms
4. Cooked rice, ham and meat
5. Soy sauce and salt

COOKING: Heat the wok, then heat 1½ tablespoons oil. Stir-fry eggs until set. Remove from the wok.

Heat the wok over medium-high heat. Heat 1 tablespoon oil. Add scallions, bean sprouts and mushrooms, and stir-fry for 1 minute. Remove and transfer to a colander.

Heat the wok, then heat 2 tablespoons oil. Add cold cooked rice, ham and meat. Stir to coat the rice with oil. Return vegetables, and add soy sauce and ¾ teaspoon salt or to taste. Stir until well mixed.

Return the cooked eggs to the wok, mixing and breaking them into small pieces. Stir and cook until rice is well heated. Serve hot.

NOTE: Leftover fried rice can be kept in the refrigerator for 3 or 4 days. Reheat the rice in a wok on the stove top, or in a microwave oven, about 1 minute per cup.

VARIATION: If lettuce or green peas are used instead of bean sprouts, add lettuce at the very end after adding the eggs, and add green peas when you add rice and meat.

Chicken and Vegetable Fried Rice

Serves 2 to 3

This delicate rice is different from subgum fried rice: instead of using cooked meat, the rice is cooked with freshly stir-fried chicken and assorted stir-fried vegetables. To contrast with the tender chicken, there are crisp carrots, red peppers and fresh snow peas, with the result as colorful as it is aromatic. You may, of course, vary the vegetables depending on what you have on hand, but try to contrast colors and textures.

½ **pound boneless, skinless chicken breast**

MARINADE:
¼ **teaspoon salt or to taste**
1½ **teaspoons cornstarch**
1 **teaspoon soy sauce**
2 **teaspoons dry sherry**
1 **teaspoon sesame oil (optional)**

5 **tablespoons cooking oil**
1 **small carrot, peeled and finely shredded**
¼ **pound fresh snow peas (about 20 medium-size ones), strings removed and finely shredded**
1 **medium-size red sweet pepper, seeded and finely shredded**
¼ **pound (about 2 cups) fresh bean sprouts, washed and drained well**
1 **clove garlic, peeled and crushed**
3 **cups cold cooked rice**
1½ **teaspoons salt or to taste**

PREPARATION: Partially frozen chicken is easier to slice by hand, or slice with medium slicing disk of food processor. Mix with the marinade.

Preparation can all be done half a day ahead.*

HAVE READY BEFORE COOKING:
1. Cooking oil
2. Chicken with marinade
3. Carrot
4. Snow peas, red pepper and bean sprouts
5. Garlic
6. Cooked rice
7. Salt

COOKING: Heat the wok over very high heat, then heat 2 tablespoons oil until very hot. Add chicken, and stir-fry until chicken just turns white. Remove chicken from the wok.

Heat 1 tablespoon oil in the same wok, and stir-fry carrot for 30 seconds to 1 minute. Add snow peas, red pepper and bean sprouts, and stir-fry for 1 to 2 minutes. Remove from the wok.

Heat 2 tablespoons oil in the wok, and fry the garlic for 30 seconds. Discard garlic. Add cold cooked rice to the hot oil. Season with 1½ teaspoons salt or to taste. Toss rice until it is coated with oil and heated through. Return vegetables and chicken to the wok and stir to mix with the rice. Serve hot.

VARIATION: Defrosted frozen French cut string beans may be used in place of snow peas. If fresh string beans are used, they should be blanched in boiling water for 2 minutes, then cut into shreds.

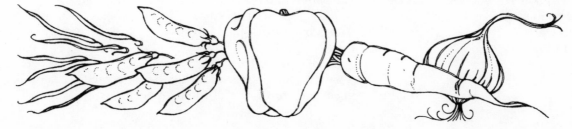

Chopped Curry Beef with Rice

Although not native to Chinese cooking, curry is ideal for spicy dishes served with rice, so this Indian spice is very popular in China and has long been used by innovative Chinese chefs. By modifying and blending it with Chinese ingredients, they have created curry dishes that are undoubtedly Chinese. Although the Chinese never prepare curry seasoning from scratch, as they do in India, curry paste and curry powder imported from India are always available in China and Chinatowns.

You may also use leftover cooked meat in this dish; just chop it coarsely with the food processor or by hand. Your family will never know this interesting dish is from yesterday's leftovers!

3 cups hot plain boiled
    rice, depending on individual's
    appetite
2 medium-size onions, peeled
1 medium-size green bell pepper,
    seeded
1 medium-size carrot, peeled
¾ pound boneless beef or pork in
    1-inch cubes, or ground meat
    without processor

MARINADE:
1 tablespoon cornstarch
1 tablespoon soy sauce
1 tablespoon dry sherry

2 tablespoons cornstarch mixed with
    ¼ cup water

4 tablespoons cooking oil
2-5 teaspoons curry powder, or
    to taste
1 tablespoon dry sherry
2 tablespoons soy sauce
1 tablespoon Worcestershire sauce
1 teaspoon sugar
¾ cup water
Salt to taste

PREPARATION: Cut each onion into quarters. With steel blade in place, chop 1 onion at a time. Remove from beaker.

Green pepper can also be chopped by processor, but you'll get better results chopping it by hand.

Cut carrot into 1-inch chunks. Then, with steel blade in place, chop with quick on/off turns. Remove from beaker.

With steel blade in place, chop meat with 3 quick on/off turns. Add marinade, and process with on/off turns until meat is coarsely chopped.

(Without food processor, chop all vegetables by hand. Use ground meat and mix with marinade by hand.*)

Mix cornstarch mixture in a bowl.*

HAVE READY BEFORE COOKING:
1. Cooking oil
2. Bowl with chopped vegetables
3. Meat with marinade
4. Seasonings and water
5. Cornstarch mixture

COOKING: Heat the wok, then heat 2 tablespoons oil until hot. Add vegetables and stir-fry about 2 minutes until onion is slightly wilted. Remove from the wok.

Heat the wok, then heat 2 tablespoons oil until very hot. Add beef, and stir-fry until beef just loses its red color. Add curry powder, sherry, soy sauce, Worcestershire sauce, sugar and water, and bring to a boil. Return vegetables to the wok.

Add cornstarch mixture, stirring constantly until sauce comes back to boiling and becomes translucent. Season to taste with salt.*

Serve with boiled rice.

VARIATION: Chopped chicken or turkey, either cooked or uncooked, may be substituted for beef.

Rice with Beef and Onion

This simple tasty dish is great for spur-of-the-moment cooking, since no unusual seasoning is necessary and most people have onions on hand. If you have some boneless beef in the freezer, you can partially defrost it in a microwave oven in no time, in about 12 minutes in a warm oven. You can further save time by slicing beef and onions with a food processor. Cooking the rice takes about 35 minutes, but if you have cooked rice on hand in the refrigerator or in the freezer, it can be rewarmed in just a few minutes in a microwave oven.

**3½ cups hot plain boiled rice,
    depending on individual's appetite**
**¾ pound flank steak or tender
    boneless beef (partially frozen for
    food processor)**

MARINADE:
1 tablespoon cornstarch
1 tablespoon dry sherry
2 tablespoons soy sauce
2 medium-size onions, peeled

SAUCE MIXTURE:
¼ teaspoon salt or to taste
¼ teaspoon ground black pepper
1 teaspoon sugar
1 tablespoon cornstarch
**1 tablespoon soy sauce (preferably
    dark soy if you have it)**
1 cup chicken broth

4 tablespoons cooking oil

PREPARATION: Pack beef snugly in the feed tube of a food processor, making sure the grain of the muscle is perpendicular to the medium slicing disk. Then slice with medium slicing disk.

(Without food processor, slice by hand to ⅛-inch-thick by 2-inch-long slices. Mix with the marinade.)

Cut ends off onions, then cut onions in half lengthwise. Place halves vertically in the feed tube and slice with medium slicing disk. Without food processor, slice by hand.

Mix sauce ingredients in a bowl.*

HAVE READY BEFORE COOKING:
1. Hot boiled rice
2. Cooking oil
3. Beef with marinade (be sure it is defrosted before cooking)
4. Onions
5. Sauce mixture

COOKING: Heat the wok until very hot, then heat 3 tablespoons oil. Add beef, and stir-fry until it just loses red color. Remove from the wok.

Heat 1 tablespoon oil in the wok. Stir-fry onions for 2 to 3 minutes over medium-high heat until soft but still crisp.

Add sauce mixture, and stir constantly until thickened. Return the beef, and stir until mixed. Serve with boiled rice.

VARIATION: Fresh tomato adds color and flavor, especially when it is vine-ripe and in season. Pour boiling water over 1 large tomato, and let stand for 1 minute. Peel off skin. Cut into wedges and remove seeds. Add tomato wedges to wok when onions are almost cooked. Cook with onions for 30 seconds, then finish cooking as in the above recipe. Add more salt to taste.

Rice with Shrimp in Sweet and Sour Sauce

Serves 4

Chinese dishes with sweet and sour sauce have long been favorites of Americans. This shrimp dish, deftly seasoned with a touch of ginger and garlic, can be cooked in two ways. A lighter dish can be made in a quicker and easier method by stir-frying the shrimp. For a more elaborate method (see Variation), the shrimp is coated with a batter and deep-fried until crisp and golden, then served with the piquant sweet and sour sauce.

3½ cups hot plain boiled
   rice, depending on individual's
   appetite
4 dry Chinese mushrooms (optional)
1 cup frozen green peas, defrosted
1 pound shrimp with shell

MARINADE:
½ teaspoon salt
½ teaspoon sugar
1 tablespoon cornstarch
2 teaspoons dry sherry

1 medium-size carrot, peeled
2 teaspoons ginger, minced
2 cloves garlic, peeled and minced
2 ounces bamboo shoots

SWEET AND SOUR SAUCE:
6 tablespoons sugar or to taste
¼ cup wine vinegar or to taste
   (or ½ cup Chinese red vinegar or
   to taste)
2 tablespoons dry sherry
2 tablespoons ketchup
2 tablespoons soy sauce
1 cup water (¾ cup if using Chinese
   red vinegar)
½ teaspoon salt or to taste

2 tablespoons cornstarch in
   ¼ cup water
4 tablespoons cooking oil

PREPARATION: Pour ½ cup boiling water over mushrooms and let soak about 20 minutes or until soft. Cut off and discard hard stems, then cut mushrooms in half.

Defrost green peas.

Shell, devein and wash the shrimp. Then drain and dry with paper towels. Mix with the marinade.

You may slice carrot with thin slicing disk of a processor, and mince garlic and ginger with steel blade, or do them by hand. Slice bamboo shoots by hand.

Mix sauce mixture in a bowl.

Combine cornstarch mixture in another bowl.*

HAVE READY BEFORE COOKING:
1. Cooking oil
2. Shrimp with marinade
3. Minced ginger and garlic
4. Sliced carrot
5. Sliced bamboo shoots and softened mushrooms
6. Sauce mixture
7. Cornstarch mixture
8. Defrosted green peas

COOKING: Heat the wok, then heat 2 tablespoons oil until very hot. Stir-fry shrimp over high heat about 2 minutes until just cooked. Time may vary depending on the size of shrimp. Do not overcook. Remove from the wok.

Heat 2 tablespoons oil over medium heat. Cook minced ginger and garlic for 30 seconds. Add carrot and stir-fry for another minute. Add bamboo shoots, mushrooms and sweet and sour sauce.

Heat until sauce comes to a boil, then add cornstarch mixture, stirring constantly until sauce is thickened. Add green peas, then return cooked shrimp and stir-fry until just heated through. Remove from heat. Serve with boiled rice.

VARIATION: Deep-fried shrimp can be used in the above recipe. Shell, devein, wash, drain and dry the shrimp. Then coat with a well-mixed, thick batter of 1 egg white, 1 teaspoon salt, 2 teaspoons dry sherry, 2 tablespoons cornstarch.

Heat 3 cups of oil at 350 degrees for deep-frying.

Just before frying, add 3 more tablespoons cornstarch to the shrimp mixture. Toss until shrimp are evenly coated.

Drop shrimp in hot oil one at a time. Do this in a few batches, making sure not to overcrowd shrimp. Fry until golden and cooked inside. Keep cooked ones in a warm oven while frying the rest.

When all the shrimp are fried, pour vegetables with sweet and sour sauce over them and serve with boiled rice.

You may substitute fresh or frozen snow peas for green peas, and ½ cup water chestnuts for bamboo shoots.

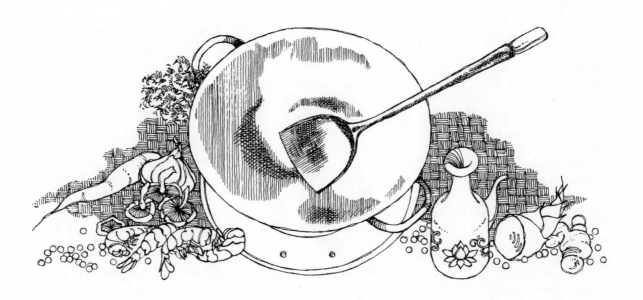

Rice with Fish in Spicy Sauce

Serves 3 to 4

Fresh fish fillets lightly coated with seasoning are quickly seared on both sides and served with a splendid spicy and garlicky brown sauce. These fish are delicious over boiled rice. The success of this dish depends largely on the freshness of the fish used. Since shopping for fish is as important as the preparation here, be sure to buy fish that are firm-textured and that do not have a fishy smell.

3½ cups hot plain boiled
   rice, depending on individual's
   appetite
1 pound boneless fillets of sea bass,
   striped bass or red snapper

MARINADE:
1 egg white
1 teaspoon ginger, finely minced
⅛ teaspoon ground black pepper
1 tablespoon cornstarch
1 tablespoon dry sherry

SAUCE MIXTURE:
1 teaspoon sugar
4 teaspoons cornstarch
1 teaspoon wine vinegar
3 tablespoons brown bean sauce,
   or to taste (or substitute soy sauce
   to taste)
1 tablespoon soy sauce (preferably
   dark soy sauce)
1 cup chicken broth

5 tablespoons cooking oil
3 dry hot red peppers, broken in
   half and seeded, or to taste (or
   1 teaspoon crushed red pepper, or
   to taste)
3 large cloves garlic, peeled and
   minced
1 tablespoon ginger, minced
2 scallions, minced

PREPARATION: Cut the fish at a slant into ½-inch-thick by 1½-inch-wide by 2-inch-long slices. Mix with the marinade.

HAVE READY BEFORE COOKING:
1. Cooking oil
2. Fish with marinade
3. Dry hot red peppers
4. Minced ginger and garlic
5. Sauce mixture
6. Minced scallion

COOKING: Heat the wok, then heat ¼ cup oil over high heat. Slide ⅓ of the fish slices, one at a time, into the hot oil. Turn over once, cooking until they are just cooked and no longer translucent. Transfer the cooked slices with a slotted spoon onto a serving platter and keep warm in the oven.

Repeat with the remaining fish slices. Keep the cooked ones warm in the oven while preparing the sauce.

Add 1 tablespoon oil to the wok. There should still be some oil left from cooking the fish; if not, add 1 more tablespoon oil, and heat on medium heat.

Fry hot pepper until just brown, then add minced garlic and ginger. Cook for 30 seconds. Do not burn garlic.

Add sauce mixture, stirring until sauce is thickened. Return fish fillets, and stir to mix. Sprinkle scallion on top. Serve with boiled rice.

Chinese Sausages with Rice

Serves 2 to 3

In Chinese cuisine, rice is usually cooked separately without any seasoning since it is to accompany other cooked dishes and will absorb their savory flavor. However, here is a dish in which rice is seasoned and cooked together with other ingredients. Chinese sausages are ideal as such ingredients. Because they are cured, even without refrigeration, they will keep for a period of time without spoiling.

Chinese sausages are smaller than their Western counterparts and more delicate in seasoning. They have a subtle, sweet flavor that is uniquely Chinese. As the rice is cooked with them, their lovely flavor and aroma gradually permeate the rice, making this a simple yet delectable dish. Accompany with a stir-fried vegetable or a soup. For variety you can use all pork sausages or mix with duck liver sausages.

4 large dry Chinese mushrooms
1 cup rice
4 Chinese sausages (about
¼ pound), sliced
1 tablespoon cooking oil
3 scallions, cut into 1-inch sections
1 teaspoon sugar
2 tablespoons soy sauce or to taste

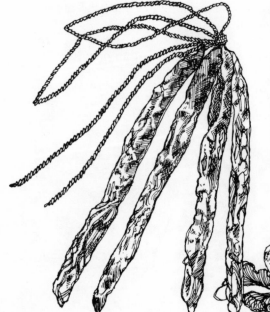

PREPARATION AND COOKING: Pour ½ cup boiling water over mushrooms and let soak about 20 minutes until soft. Cut off and discard hard stems, then cut mushrooms into smaller pieces.

Wash rice with cold water in the saucepan you are going to use for cooking. Stir rice, then drain in a strainer. Repeat 2 times. Drain the rice very well.

Return rice to the saucepan, and add 1½ cups water. Bring to a boil on high heat, then lower to medium heat and cook rice uncovered until most of the water has evaporated. Scatter sliced sausages and cut up mushrooms evenly on top of the rice.

Cover the saucepan, and let cook on very low heat for about 15 minutes. Turn off heat and let stand for 10 minutes. Do not remove the cover.

In the meantime, heat the wok, then heat 1 tablespoon of oil in the wok. Add scallions and stir-fry for about 1 minute. Remove from heat and add sugar and soy sauce. Stir to dissolve the sugar, if necessary. Heat slowly on low heat.

Pour the scallion mixture onto the cooked rice, and toss to mix. Serve hot.

Stuffed Bean Curd

Makes 8 triangles

This bean curd dish is commonly served as dim sum in the teahouses. However, you can also serve it as a main dish; with boiled rice and a green vegetable it makes a nutritious and inexpensive meal, for bean curd is high in protein but low in fat, calories and cholesterol.

Bean curd is made from soybean milk. Cream-colored and rather bland in taste, it readily absorbs the flavor of the ingredients with which it is cooked. There are soft and hard bean curds. For this dish, use the hard variety that is sold in 3-inch squares, about 1 inch thick. The hard bean curd sold in a 1-pound block will not work well.

FILLING:

1 tablespoon dry shrimp
2 dry Chinese mushrooms
1 scallion, cut to 2-inch sections
1 cube fresh ginger, ½ inch (about 1 teaspoon minced)
2 ounces boneless pork in 1-inch cubes, or ground pork without processor
¼ teaspoon salt or to taste
Dash ground black pepper or to taste
1 teaspoon cornstarch
2 teaspoons soy sauce
1 teaspoon sesame oil (optional)

4 pieces hard bean curd (about 3 by 3 by ¾ inches)
3 tablespoons cooking oil

PREPARATION: Soak dry shrimp and mushrooms separately in 2 small bowls with boiling water until soft, about 10 minutes for shrimp and 20 minutes for mushrooms. Cut off and discard hard stems from mushrooms, then cut mushrooms in half or in quarters.

With steel blade in place, mince scallion and ginger until very fine. Add pork cubes, and chop with 2 quick on/off turns. Add softened shrimp and mushrooms, and remaining filling ingredients. Process until ingredients are minced.*

(Without food processor, mince softened shrimp and mushrooms to the size of rice, and ginger and scallions until very fine. Mix by hand with ground pork and all remaining ingredients for filling.*)

Cut each bean curd square into 2 equal triangles. Drain well and blot dry with paper towels. Cut an opening along

SAUCE:

¼ cup chicken broth

2 tablespoons or more water

1 tablespoon oyster-flavored sauce
   (or soy sauce to taste)

1 tablespoon soy sauce or to taste

⅛ teaspoon ground black pepper or
   to taste

1 teaspoon cornstarch mixed with
   1 tablespoon water

2 teaspoons sesame oil (optional)

1 scallion, finely minced

the longest side of each triangle and make a pocket. Do not cut through the other 2 sides.

Divide the filling into 8 equal portions. Fill each portion in a pocket and smooth filling out along the openings.*

COOKING: Heat the wok, then heat 3 tablespoons oil until very hot. Fry bean curds on both sides until golden. Fry in 2 batches.*

Place bean curds in a standard or a heat-to-serve pot. Add chicken broth, water, oyster-flavored sauce and soy sauce. Bring to a boil, then let simmer for 7 to 8 minutes or until filling is cooked. Add more water if the liquid is evaporating too fast. Add ground pepper, then thicken the sauce with the cornstarch mixture. Add sesame oil, and garnish with minced scallion. Serve hot.*

NOTE: The dish can be rewarmed on the stove top or in a microwave oven.

Egg Noodles, Wonton, Cantonese Egg Roll and Steamed Dumpling Wrappers

Makes 1 pound

Although the Chinese frequently use fresh noodles and wrappers of wontons and dumplings, it is not a practice to make them at home, since they are easily available from noodle factories. With the growing popularity of Chinese food in the United States, noodle factories are flourishing in Chinatowns of large American cities, and supply American supermarkets, as well as Oriental food stores, with noodles and wrappers.

These ready-made noodles and wrappers are sold in 1-pound packages. They can be kept in the refrigerator for two to three days, or in the freezer for many months, so it is worthwhile to buy extra amounts and divide them into smaller packages to freeze for future use. Noodles don't have to be defrosted before cooking, so they are an especially practical staple for short-notice cooking.

If you do decide to make your own noodles and wrappers, here is a recipe.

2 cups all-purpose flour

¼ teaspoon salt or to taste

1 large egg

About ½ cup water, depending on
   the flour

Cornstarch for dusting

PREPARATION: With steel blade or short plastic dough blade in place, mix flour and salt. With the machine running, add egg, and pour in about three-quarters of the water. Then dribble in remaining water only until a ball of dough forms. Keep the machine running for another minute. The dough should be a little sticky but not wet. Add more flour or water if necessary.

(Without food processor, mix all the ingredients by hand until dough is formed, then knead for 10 minutes or until dough is smooth.)

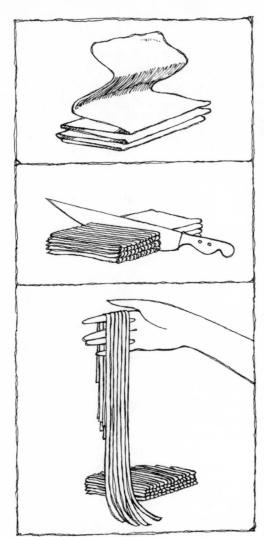

Transfer the dough to a bowl and cover with plastic wrap. Let it rest for 30 minutes.*

ROLLING: Dust your working surface with cornstarch. Divide the dough into 2 portions. Roll each portion out to a 1/16-inch-thick sheet or to a sheet of your desired thickness, with a rolling pin. (You can use a pasta machine for rolling and shaping.)

Let the sheets stand for 30 to 60 minutes until dried to a semi-stiff state. (You can also hang them over the backs of two chairs to dry.) The sheets should not be limp or stretchable, nor should they crack when folded.

SHAPING: With a cleaver or sharp knife, cut 7-inch squares for Cantonese egg roll wrappers, and 3-inch squares for wonton wrappers. With a cookie-cutter, cut rounds 3 inches in diameter for steamed dumpling wrappers. Sprinkle a little cornstarch in between wrappers before stacking to prevent sticking.

To make noodles, dust both sides of the dough sheets with cornstarch, then fold accordion-style into 3-inch-wide folds. With cleaver or sharp knife, cut across folds into 1/16-inch strips or to your desired width, making sure to cut all the way through dough. Fluff the noodles up with your fingers. They are ready to be cooked. Or sprinkle with more cornstarch to keep for later use.*

NOTE: Wrappers and noodles can be stored in well-sealed plastic bags in the refrigerator for 2 to 3 days or in the freezer for several months. The wrappers should be completely defrosted before using.

Soft-Fried Noodles with Roast Pork

Serves 2 to 3

To the Chinese, chow mein means stir-fried noodles. Unfortunately, for a long time Americanized Chinese restaurants have served short crunchy deep-fried noodles and called them "chow mein." These are very inferior in quality and taste to stir-fried noodles and are unknown in China.

Stir-fried noodles are delicious and can be cooked with a variety of meat, chicken, seafood and vegetables. Chinese fresh egg noodles are excellent for stir-frying; however, dry noodles, extra-thin spaghetti from American supermarkets, or any homemade noodles can be substituted. To get best results, the noodles should not be overcooked. They should be tender but still somewhat chewy, yet resistant to the bite.

The amount of noodles used per serving depends largely on individual appetite, and on whether you are a noodle lover like the northern Chinese. A half pound of noodles after boiling yields about four cups, which will feed two to four people.

4 dry Chinese mushrooms
¾ pound celery cabbage or bok choy
½ pound Chinese Roast Pork (see page 48)
½ pound fresh Chinese egg noodles or dry substitutes
5 tablespoons cooking oil
2 slices fresh ginger
2 scallions cut into 2-inch sections, then shredded
¼ teaspoon salt or to taste
2 tablespoons soy sauce or to taste (or use oyster sauce to taste)

PREPARATION AND COOKING: Pour ½ cup boiling water over mushrooms and let soak for 20 minutes or until soft.

Bring 2 quarts of water to boil in a large pot while preparing the other steps.

Wash cabbage or bok choy. Be sure to remove sandy particles. Cut stems into 2-inch sections, then cut into ¼-inch shreds. Cut leaves into ¼-inch-wide strips.

The food processor does not slice or shred cooked meat neatly, so cut roast pork by hand into ⅛-inch-thick slices, then cut into ¼-inch-wide by 2-inch-long shreds.

Cut off and discard hard stems from softened mushrooms, then cut mushrooms into ⅛-inch shreds.*

When the water is boiling, add fresh noodles and cook for 1 to 2 minutes. (Cook dry noodles or spaghetti according to package instructions.) Do not overcook; noodles should be somewhat resistant to the bite. Drain immediately in a colander and rinse with cold water. Drain very well. If noodles are not to be used right away, toss them with 1 tablespoon of oil to prevent sticking.

Heat wok, then heat 2 tablespoons oil. Fry ginger until golden and remove from oil. Add scallions, cabbage, mushrooms and ¼ teaspoon salt or to taste. Add roast pork just to heat through. Remove from the wok.

Heat the wok, then heat 3 tablespoons oil on medium heat. Add the noodles and stir constantly about 2 minutes until heated through and coated with oil. You may find it easier to cut the noodles for stir-frying.

Return meat and vegetables to the wok and mix with noodles. Add soy sauce to taste, stirring until noodles become one even color. Serve hot.

VARIATION: You may substitute stir-fried meat for pork, and Swiss chard, fresh snow peas, or fresh bean sprouts for vegetable.

Crispy Pan-Fried Noodles

In Shanghai this is called "two sides golden fried noodles." The noodles are precooked, then pan-fried until both sides are golden and crispy but the inside is still soft. Then they are topped with stir-fried meat and vegetables, along with a glazed sauce that flavors the noodles, making their outsides slightly soft but still crisp in texture. This is one of my family's favorite noodle dishes. Our cook in Shanghai used to make this as an afternoon snack, especially when company was coming. In those days, guests were invited for afternoon snacks as well as dinner. Most would come early in the afternoon to play mahjong, a popular pastime in China, and many continued the game after dinner, often until late in the night.

Although this dish is more involved than most other noodle dishes in this book, the preparation can be done several hours ahead, and the result is well worth the effort. It is a unique Chinese creation, to taste noodles both soft and crispy at one time in one dish. You will get the best results using Chinese fresh egg noodles.

**½ pound fresh Chinese egg noodles
  or dry noodles**
5 dry Chinese mushrooms
½ pound shrimp with shells

MARINADE FOR SHRIMP:
1 teaspoon cornstarch
¼ teaspoon salt
½ teaspoon sugar
1 teaspoon dry sherry

**½ pound boneless, skinless chicken
  breast**

MARINADE FOR CHICKEN:
1½ teaspoons cornstarch
½ teaspoon salt
2 teaspoons dry sherry

**¾ pound bok choy or
  celery cabbage**
3 scallions

PREPARATION: Cook noodles in 2 quarts of boiling water for 1 to 2 minutes until soft but still resistant to the bite. Quickly drain in colander and rinse with cold water. Drain very well. Then let stand in air until ready to cook. Noodles will be crisper when fried and taste better if you can boil them several hours ahead.

Pour ½ cup boiling water over mushrooms and let soak about 20 minutes or until soft. Cut off and discard hard stems, then cut mushrooms into smaller pieces.

Shell, devein and wash shrimp. Then drain and pat dry with paper towels. Mix with the shrimp marinade.

With medium slicing disk, slice partially frozen chicken across the grain. (Without food processor, slice chicken by hand across the grain.) Mix with the chicken marinade.

Wash bok choy or celery cabbage. Remove any sandy particles. Cut into ¼-inch-wide by 2-inch-long strips. Cut scallions into 2-inch sections, then cut into shreds.

Mix sauce ingredients in small bowl.

HAVE READY BEFORE COOKING:
1. 1 cup cooking oil
2. Cold boiled noodles
3. Shrimp with marinade
4. Chicken with marinade
5. Bok choy, mushrooms, scallions; place ginger slices on top
6. Sauce mixture
7. Sesame oil (optional)

SAUCE MIXTURE:
5 teaspoons cornstarch
1 tablespoon oyster-flavored sauce
  (or use soy sauce to taste)
1 tablespoon soy sauce or to taste
½ teaspoon sugar
1¼ cups chicken broth

½ cup cooking oil
2 slices fresh ginger
1 tablespoon sesame oil

COOKING: Heat the wok, then heat ½ cup oil until just beginning to haze. Gently drop the noodles in the hot oil and fry until golden and crisp on 1 side. Then turn over and fry the other side until it is golden and crisp, about 5 to 10 minutes, depending on your heat. Drain noodles on paper towels. Transfer to a serving platter and keep warm in the oven.

Remove all but 1½ tablespoons oil and heat the wok. Stir-fry shrimp about 1 to 2 minutes until it is just cooked. Remove from the wok.

Heat 2 tablespoons oil in the wok. Stir-fry chicken about 2 minutes until it just turns white. Remove from the wok.

Heat 2 tablespoons oil in the wok and fry ginger slices until golden. Discard ginger. Stir-fry bok choy or cabbage, mushrooms and scallions for 1 to 2 minutes. Add sauce mixture, stirring until thick and translucent. Add chicken and shrimp to heat through. Season to taste, add sesame oil, then pour on top of the warm noodles and serve immediately. You may find it easier to serve by cutting the fried noodles into wedges before putting the sauce on.

VARIATION: You may use all shrimp or all chicken instead of both. You can substitute fresh snow peas or sliced bamboo shoots for vegetable.

Aromatic Beef Noodles

Serves 3 as one-dish meal, 6 as snack

The Chinese often serve noodles in a bowl of soup and top it with meat and vegetables. This is called soup noodles, and it can be served as a between-meal snack or a full meal. Aromatic Beef Noodles is modified from a well-known soup noodles recipe of the Szechuan region where the soup is cooked with hot bean sauce. The subtle and aromatic soup in this recipe is equally good without the hot flavor, with hot chili oil added instead at the table. The beef and soup can be cooked several days ahead and in large quantity, then served with freshly cooked noodles.

2 tablespoons cooking oil
4 slices fresh ginger
5 cloves garlic, peeled
1 pound boneless beef chuck, cut into 1-inch cubes
5 cups water
2 tablespoons sugar
5 tablespoons brown bean sauce or to taste
¼ cup dry sherry
2 whole star anise
1 tablespoon Szechuan peppercorns
Salt to taste
Soy sauce to taste
¾ to 1 pound fresh egg noodles (or dry noodles or dry extra thin spaghetti)
2 cloves garlic (optional), mashed into paste or crushed through a garlic press
2 tablespoons sesame oil or to taste (optional)
1 large scallion, finely minced
Hot chili oil to taste (optional) (or use Tabasco sauce, or Chinese chili paste)

COOKING: Heat oil in a 3-quart saucepan, fry ginger and garlic for 30 seconds, then add beef. Cook until beef loses its red color. Add water, sugar, brown bean sauce and sherry. Place star anise and Szechuan peppercorns in a stainless steel tea strainer or tie them in a cheesecloth bag, then place them in the saucepan.

Cook for 1½ to 2 hours until beef is tender. Add salt or soy sauce to taste. There are about 4 cups of soup in the saucepan. Remove spice bag.*

In another pot, cook fresh egg noodles for about 2 minutes or until just cooked. Do not overcook. (Cook spaghetti according to the package directions.) Quickly drain noodles in a colander. They should be soft but resistant to the bite.

Add garlic paste to the simmering soup just before serving. Add sesame oil, and remove from heat.

Place noodles and soup in a tureen, or dish into individual bowls. Garnish with minced scallions. Let each diner add hot chili oil to taste.

Soup Noodles with Chicken

To satisfy light hunger pangs, the Chinese often cook up quick and simple soup noodles. They make a good snack or a light meal. The noodles are usually served in individual bowls with clear broth.

The sizes of the bowl and the quantity of noodles served can vary according to individual appetites, and there is no limit to what to use as noodle toppings. This is a wonderful way of using leftovers such as roast chicken, turkey or ham. Since the noodles are comparatively bland in themselves, the broth used should have a good flavor.

4 dry Chinese mushrooms (optional)
4 to 6 cups chicken broth,
    homemade or canned
½ pound cooked chicken, ham or
    turkey, or an assortment of them
12 to 18 fresh snow peas
½ pound fresh or dry noodles, or
    extra thin spaghetti
1 slice fresh ginger
Salt to taste
1 tablespoon sesame oil (optional)

PREPARATION AND COOKING: Pour ½ cup boiling water over mushrooms and let soak about 20 minutes or until soft. Squeeze mushrooms dry, cut off and discard hard stems, then cut mushrooms in half. Save the juice from mushrooms for it will add flavor when combined with chicken broth.

Bring 2 quarts of water to a boil in large pot. In another pot, bring chicken broth with mushroom juice to a boil.

While the water and chicken broth are being heated, slice the meat very thinly by hand. Remove hard strings from snow peas, then wash and drain.

Cook noodles in boiling water just until soft but still a little chewy to the bite. Add 2 cups of cold water to stop the water from boiling. Quickly drain the noodles in a colander. Place noodles in a large soup tureen or divide into individual bowls.

Add ginger, mushrooms and snow peas to the boiling chicken broth and cook for 1 minute. Salt to taste, and add sesame oil. Remove from heat.

Place meat slices on top of noodles in tureen or individual bowls, then pour chicken broth over the noodles, and top with the vegetables. Serve hot.

VARIATION: You may substitute fresh spinach or sliced bamboo shoots for snow peas.

Stir-Fried Rice Sticks with Beef

Serves 3

Most Americans are familiar with the more common types of Chinese noodles made from wheat flour, but they are generally not knowledgeable about noodles made from rice powder. The dried ones used in this recipe come in white, thin and slightly wavy sticks—hence the derivation of the name rice sticks. They are most popular in the south, where rice is abundant.

Only a brief soaking is necessary before stir-frying. Stir-fried rice sticks have a lighter quality than the wheat flour noodles. Since dry rice sticks will keep indefinitely in a cool, dry place, they are wonderful staples to keep on hand for quick impromptu meals, and are easily available at Oriental stores or from mail-order sources.

6 ounces rice sticks
¾ pound flank steak or tender boneless beef (partially frozen)

MARINADE:
1 tablespoon cornstarch
1 tablespoon dry sherry
2 tablespoons soy sauce

½ pound celery cabbage, bok choy or fresh bean sprouts
4 scallions
5 tablespoons cooking oil
2 slices fresh ginger
1 clove garlic, peeled
2 tablespoons oyster-flavored sauce (or soy sauce to taste)
1 tablespoon soy sauce
Salt to taste if desired

PREPARATION: Soak rice sticks in lukewarm water for about 15 minutes until pliable but still a little chewy. Do not oversoak, for they will get too soft. Drain in a colander. This can be done many hours ahead.*

Pack partially frozen beef in the feed tube of a food processor, so it will slice across the grain with medium slicing disk. (Without food processor, slice by hand to ⅛-inch-thick by 2-inch-long slices.) Mix with the marinade.

If celery cabbage or bok choy is used, cut into ¼-inch shreds. Cut scallions into 1½-inch sections.*

HAVE READY BEFORE COOKING:
1. Bottle of cooking oil
2. Beef in bowl with ginger and garlic on top
3. Vegetable and scallions
4. Softened rice sticks
5. Oyster sauce, soy sauce and salt

COOKING: Heat the wok, then heat 3 tablespoons oil. Fry ginger and garlic for 40 seconds until light golden. Remove from oil. Add beef, and stir-fry on high heat until beef just loses its red color. Remove from wok.

Heat 2 tablespoons oil in the wok. Stir-fry vegetables and scallions for 1 to 2 minutes. Add rice sticks, then oyster sauce and soy sauce, stirring to mix until rice sticks are heated.

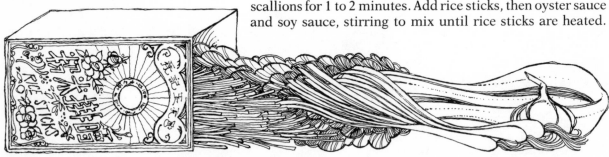

Return beef, and stir to mix. Taste for seasoning, add salt or more soy sauce if desired. Serve hot.

VARIATION: You may substitute green bell pepper for vegetable, pork or chicken for beef.

Rice Sticks, Singapore-Style
Serves 3

This exotic curry-flavored dish originated in Singapore, but is very popular with the Chinese and is always available in the teahouses. Singapore, which is at the southern tip of the Malay Peninsula, has a very large Chinese population, and, needless to say, Singapore cooking is influenced by the Chinese. Often Singapore dishes are blends of Chinese, Indian and Malayan spices and ingredients. The results are interesting assortments of colors, textures and flavors, as reflected in this dish.

¼ pound rice sticks (also called rice vermicelli)
½ pound Chinese roast pork (or cooked ham)

SHRIMP MIXTURE:
½ pound shrimp with shell
1 teaspoon cornstarch
¼ teaspoon salt
1 teaspoon dry sherry

1 red bell pepper
1 medium-size onion, peeled
3 eggs
4 tablespoons cooking oil
½ pound fresh bean sprouts, washed and drained (or shredded celery cabbage)
¼ cup chicken broth
1 tablespoon curry powder or to taste
2 tablespoons soy sauce or to taste
1 teaspoon sugar
½ teaspoon salt or to taste

PREPARATION: Soak rice sticks in lukewarm water for about 15 minutes until pliable but still a little chewy. Do not oversoak, for they will get too soft. Drain in a colander. This can be done many hours ahead.*

Shred roast pork or ham by hand.

Shell, devein and wash shrimp. Then drain and pat dry with paper towels. Split shrimp into halves and mix with the remaining 3 ingredients for shrimp mixture.

Cut top off red pepper, remove seeds, then cut lengthwise into 2-inch sections. Cut onion in half lengthwise. Then cut pepper and onion into shreds by hand or with medium slicing disk of a processor.*

HAVE READY BEFORE COOKING:
1. Cooking oil
2. 3 eggs
3. Shrimp mixture
4. Bean sprouts, onion and pepper
5. Chicken broth
6. Curry powder, soy sauce, sugar and salt
7. Rice sticks and pork

COOKING: Beat 1 egg in a small bowl. Heat the wok, then heat 1 teaspoon oil over medium heat. Add the egg, and swirl around the wok to form a pancake about 9 inches in diameter. Cook until the egg is set. Lift the pancake from the wok. Repeat process with the other 2 eggs, then shred all the eggs by hand. This can be done many hours ahead.*

Heat the wok, then heat 2 tablespoons oil. Stir-fry shrimp for 1 to 2 minutes until just cooked. Remove from wok.

Heat 2 tablespoons oil in the same wok. Stir-fry bean sprouts, onion and pepper for 1 to 2 minutes. Add chicken broth, curry powder, soy sauce, sugar and salt to taste. Heat to boiling. Add rice sticks and meat. Return shrimp and egg shreds. Toss to mix until the rice sticks are heated through. Serve hot.

VARIATION: Chicken may be substituted for shrimp.

Fresh Rice Noodles with Beef (*Beef Chow Fun*)

Soft, white, wide fresh rice noodles have a smooth and slippery texture. They readily absorb the flavor of other ingredients and can be cooked with a variety of meat and vegetables. Delicious and different from other noodles, they are popular and standard fare in teahouses or Cantonese restaurants.

The easiest way to cook fresh rice noodles at home is to purchase ready-made fresh rice noodles ahead of time in Chinatown or at those local Oriental food stores that carry them, then keep in the freezer, and just defrost before cooking. Do not confuse these noodles with rice sticks, which are dry and brittle thin sticks that have to be soaked and softened before using.

4 dry Chinese mushrooms (optional)
¾ pound flank steak or tender boneless beef

MARINADE:
1 tablespoon cornstarch
2 tablespoons soy sauce
1 tablespoon dry sherry

5 tablespoons cooking oil
1 clove garlic, peeled
¾ pound fresh bean sprouts, washed and drained (or shredded celery cabbage or bok choy)
4 scallions, cut into 2-inch shreds
1 pound fresh rice noodles
3 tablespoons soy sauce
½ teaspoon sugar
½ teaspoon salt or to taste

PREPARATION: Pour ½ cup boiling water over mushrooms and let soak for 20 minutes or until soft. Cut off and discard hard stems. Then cut mushrooms into smaller pieces.

Slice beef across the grain into ⅛-inch-thick by 2-inch-long slices either by hand or with medium slicing disk of a processor. Partially frozen beef is easier to slice by hand, or it can be sliced with the medium slicing disk of a processor.

Mix beef with the marinade.

If the rice noodles are in sheets, cut in ½-inch strips.*

HAVE READY BEFORE COOKING:
1. Cooking oil
2. Beef with marinade
3. Garlic
4. Bean sprouts, scallions and softened mushrooms
5. Rice noodles
6. Soy sauce, sugar and salt

COOKING: Heat the wok over high heat, then heat 3 tablespoons oil until very hot. Add beef, and stir-fry about 2 minutes, until beef just loses red color. Remove from wok.

Heat 2 tablespoons oil in the wok. Fry garlic for about 1 minute, then discard. Add bean sprouts, scallions and mushrooms, and cook for 1 minute. Add rice noodles and toss to mix. Return beef and add soy sauce, sugar and salt to taste. Toss and mix until the noodles are heated through. Serve hot.

VARIATION: You can substitute ¾ pound of fresh broccoli for bean sprouts and scallions. Cut off florets from stems. (Cut about 1½ inches from top of floret into stem.) Then cut large florets into pieces about ½ inch by ½ inch on the top of floret. Cut off tough bottoms from stems of broccoli and discard. Peel skin off stems, then slice stems by hand or with medium slicing disk.

Tea

For centuries tea has been the most popular beverage in China. People drink it from morning to evening. It is a part of daily life, and a part of Chinese culture.

Tea is also a means of expressing hospitality and friendship. Visitors are always served a cup of hot tea, regardless of the time of day or season of the year. This practice is still very prevalent in China today, as my family and I noticed when we went back to visit recently. Everywhere we went sightseeing, we were served hot tea before starting on our tour. And every hotel room supplied us with tea and hot

water in a thermos bottle, so we could have hot tea any time of the day. I noticed, too, that the Chinese now also have tea bags—a Western idea they have adopted!

Chinese people bring tea for gifts just as Westerners bring wine. Tea is usually packed in colorful canisters or containers, and there are shops that specialize in and sell only tea. The quality of it varies just as wine does. Good tea can be very expensive and makes a very special gift.

In China, tea is served before and after, but not during the meal, for soup is considered the beverage. The only exception to this is at teahouses, where tea is, in fact, the only beverage served with dim sum. At the teahouse you can choose your tea. And, as with wine, the only way to find out which tea you like is by tasting and trying the many varieties. In general, tea can be divided into three groups.

Green tea, also known as *unfermented tea*, is roasted right after picking, giving it a pure and refreshing taste. The best known is called Loong Ching, which means "Dragon Well" in Chinese; others are Gunpowder and Lu An.

Red tea, known as *black tea* in America, is a *fermented tea*. The brew is much darker in color than green tea and has a stronger flavor. Two popular ones are Keman and Iron Goddess of Mercy.

Semi-fermented tea is in between green and black tea in flavor and color. The leaves are roasted after partial fermentation. The most popular one is Oolong.

There is also *scented tea*, such as chrysanthemum tea; jasmine tea, which is Oolong tea with jasmine blossoms; and lychee tea, which is black tea with a sweet touch of lychee fruit. The *smoked tea*, Lapsang Souchong, is less popular in China.

TO BREW TEA:

For average tea taste, use 1 teaspoon tea leaves to ¾ measuring cup (1 cup in a cup and saucer) of freshly boiled water. Let it steep for 3 to 4 minutes before serving. The Chinese brew tea to the individual's taste, so use more tea if you like it stronger, less if you like it weaker. Strong tea can also be diluted with hot water. It is not a Chinese custom to use sugar and cream in tea.

Tea should be steeped in porcelain teacups or teapot. Do not use metal pots, as they will distort the flavor.

Menu Suggestions for Entertaining

Although the cocktail party is a Western phenomenon, the following dim sum will adapt very well as hors d'oeuvres. They will bring a new taste sensation to your party with the advantage that they can be made ahead and rewarmed before serving. You can serve as many varieties as you wish, but even just one can set the pace or be a main feature, and blend harmoniously with your Western food.

FOOD TO BE REWARMED IN 350-DEGREE OVEN
Shrimp Rolls
Fried Shrimp Sandwiches
Miniature Pear-Shaped Dumplings
Taro Crescents
Roast Pork in Flaky Pastry
Curry Puffs

FOOD TO BE STEAMED
Crab Meat and Shrimp Dumplings
Glutinous Rice Dumplings
Steamed Beef Balls
Steamed Shrimp Dumplings

FOOD TO BE FRIED
Spring Rolls (to serve, cut in half after cooking)

If you feel ambitious and would like to have a dim sum party to impress your guests, plan your menu with variety: a variety of foods, a variety of seasonings, and a variety of cooking methods. If you have a dish that is to be steamed, then plan a reheated one next in the oven, so both can be heated at the same time. Since most dim sum can be cooked ahead, plan and organize to pace yourself, by preparing the food far in advance so you can relax and enjoy the party. Since all these foods can be made in large quantities, you can serve as many people as you wish, but keep in mind what you can comfortably handle with your experience, your facilities and your equipment. You can serve one or a few dim sum at a time, or spread the food out in buffet style, letting the guests help themselves and freeing yourself from running back and forth to the kitchen. Reheat the food just before serving, and keep warm on hot plates or keep steamed food warm in the steamer. In Chinatowns, you can find inexpensive shallow bamboo steamers, and can buy as many as four or five tiers (12 inches to 13 inches in diameter) that fit one over another onto an electric wok. The wok will heat and keep warm all five tiers of food, and it makes a good-looking serving piece for your buffet table.

The following menu suggestions are planned with variety in mind. You may use fewer or more recipes depending on the number of people and how elaborate a party you want, or substitute other recipes to suit your taste and the equipment you have. Each individual recipe gives information on reheating and storage for advanced preparation.

MENU I
Fried Shrimp Sandwiches—reheat in 350-degree oven
Steamed Beef Balls—prepare in advance; cook in steamer
Spring Rolls—cook or refry in oil just before serving
Tea
Fruit, or Coconut Tarts—serve at room temperature or warm by reheating in oven

MENU II
Miniature Pear-Shaped Dumplings—reheat in 350-degree oven
Crab Meat and Shrimp Dumplings—prepare in advance and steam
Stuffed Bean Curd—cook in advance and rewarm on stove top or in microwave oven
Subgum Fried Rice—cook just before serving, or cook ahead and rewarm
Tea
Fruit

MENU III
Shrimp Rolls—reheat in 350-degree oven
Curry Puffs (beef)—reheat in 350-degree oven
Steamed Roast Pork Buns—reheat in the steamer
Glutinous Rice Dumplings—prepare in advance and steam
Tea
Fruit

MENU IV
Roast Pork in Flaky Pastry—reheat in 350-degree oven
Steamed Shrimp Dumplings—prepare in advance and steam
Rice Sticks, Singapore-Style—can be cooked ahead and rewarmed, but tastes best when freshly cooked. Preparation and some part of cooking can be done ahead, so last-minute cooking is only a few minutes.
Tea
Fruit, or Steamed Red Bean Paste Buns—prepare in advance and resteam

Mail-Order Sources

A recent survey I did on Chinese mail-order sources showed that in many states there are individual Chinese groceries that will mail ingredients upon request, but none of them has price lists or order forms. You have to write or call to get information, and often the clerks working in these groceries do not speak much English.

There are two places I know of, however, that are strictly mail-order houses and specialize exclusively in Chinese cooking items. The staff at both houses speaks English and offers reliable service, plus detailed, well-organized price lists and order forms. Both stock Chinese cooking utensils as well as ingredients, and will mail items that may not be on their order forms.

The Chinese Kitchen
P.O. Box 218
Stirling, New Jersey 07980

The Chinese Grocer
209 Post Street
San Francisco, California 94108